THE OLYMPIC PENINSULA

ERICKA CHICKOWSKI

Contents

THE OLYMPIC PENINSULA

OLYMPIC PENINSULA AND THE COAST

Washington's Olympic Peninsula juts up like a thumb hitchhiking a ride from Canada. This diverse 6,500-square-mile landmass ranges from remote rocky beaches to subalpine meadows, from majestic glacier-faced mountains to spooky rainforests. One of the most remarkable parts of the state, the peninsula has a rugged and wild beauty that embodies the spirit of the Evergreen State as much as any place in Washington. The beating heart of the peninsula is Olympic National Park, an unspoiled forest rich with old growth trees, wildlife, and awe-inspiring vistas. Beyond the park, the peninsula lives by the chainsaw, with lumber still providing paychecks for local residents. Tree farms abound, many with signs indicating when they were last cut and when the next round of logging will take place. The large trucks hauling massive cut logs are a common sight.

© WASHINGTON STATE TOURISM

THE OLYMPIC PENINSULA **9**

HIGHLIGHTS

◖ Dosewallips State Park: Hike, swim, fish, or clam at this recreational centerpiece where the Dosewallips River meets the Hood Canal (page 19).

◖ Fort Worden State Park: Explore underground bunkers, an airship balloon hangar, and even a marine science center in this

park on the northeast corner of the Olympic Peninsula (page 26).

◖ Dungeness Spit: Walk the longest naturally occurring sand spit in the United States all the way to the end and reward yourself with a tour of the historic lighthouse (page 34).

◖ Hurricane Ridge: Peer over at Canada, Seattle, and even Mount Hood atop this amazing viewpoint. In the summer, the wildflowers abound here (page 42).

◖ Lake Crescent: Explore the vividly colored lake by boat, or just take a hike by the shore (page 50).

◖ Sol Duc Hot Springs: Nothing beats a post-hike soak in Washington's most famous hot springs (page 52).

◖ Rialto Beach Area: The towering sea stacks dotted with evergreens, the enormous blanched driftwood logs, and the thundering surf all make for a dramatic visit to this stretch of shoreline (page 59).

◖ Hoh Rain Forest: Who says rainforests are only in South America? Bring a slicker and enjoy the magnificently mossy trees and shrouds of ferns covering this forest (page 60).

◖ Lake Quinault: Take a hike through the old-growth forest that surrounds this showcase of the Quinault Valley (page 63).

◖ Cape Disappointment State Park: Sitting at the mouth of the Columbia River, this is the most impressive of all the state parks, offering museums, beaches, wooded trails, lighthouses, and military history galore (page 84).

◖ Willapa Bay: Hunt for oysters, kayak the flats, and explore the islands at one of the nation's most pristine estuaries (page 87).

LOOK FOR ◖ TO FIND RECOMMENDED SIGHTS, ACTIVITIES, DINING, AND LODGING.

Olympic National Park

Hard-core hikers and campers who think they've seen it all will never forget the wonder of the Olympic National Park, even after just one visit. The deep, damp rain forests, the frosted mountaintops, the aquamarine rivers have a fantastical allure, seeming to leap from the pages of storybooks. Auto roads barely penetrate the park, but more than 600 miles of hiking trails meander through, crossing and connecting the park's virgin forest core, its matchless beaches, and its alpine peaks.

Olympic National Park is probably most famous for the lush rain forests that carpet the western flanks of the mountains. The best known and most visited is Hoh Rain Forest, but the others—Quinault and Queets—are fascinating, too, and visitors are more likely to have a more personal experience. Soaking up the ample rainfall, enormous spruce, cedar, fir, and hemlock trees covered with moss and lichen tower over the traveler, forcing a certain degree of perspective on life. The crystal-clear rivers and streams, the thick scent of fertility, and the tickle of mist on your eyelashes give this forest an unforgettable feeling of enchantment.

The diversity of climate and geography in Olympic National Park's 908,720 acres of wilderness is one of many reasons it was among the 100 parks named a World Heritage Park by the United Nations in 1981. The largest old-growth coniferous forest in the Lower 48 states, the park is home to 200 species of birds and 70 species of mammals, including Roosevelt elk, black bear, deer, bald eagles, and Olympic marmots. Today Olympic National Park sees over four million visitors a year. Despite its popularity, the park's size and hard-to-reach interior mean it's not hard to find peaceful solitude on the many lakes and trails.

HISTORY

American Indian tribes once sparsely inhabited the land now known as the Olympic Peninsula; evidence of their presence here dates back thousands of years. Coastal tribes lived off of the once-abundant salmon or hunted the Pacific gray whale, a tradition still practiced by treaty right by the Makah Tribe today. Starting in the 16th century, the region attracted the attention first of the Spanish, then the English, and finally, Americans. Due to the unforgiving landscape and the frequently hostile Makah, white settlement didn't take hold until 1851, although the Spanish briefly held a fort here and trappers and explorers plied their trades in the area much earlier.

Coastal settlements sprang up here and there, but few dared enter the thick forests and steep slopes of the central Olympics. This situation changed in 1889 when the *Seattle Press* newspaper funded a small party of adventurers and tasked them with exploring the hinterland. The trip went about as well as can be expected from an excursion organized by the media. Plagued by poor planning, a brutal winter, and a string of mishaps, the group took six months to travel across the mountains before arriving on the Quinalt Indian Reservation—starving, minus two mules and several dogs, and in desperate need of medical attention.

Seven years after the *Press* expedition, Congress created the Olympic Forest Reserve, which included much of the Olympic Peninsula. In 1909 President Theodore Roosevelt set aside much of the area for conservation by naming it Mount Olympus National Monument, and in 1938 President Franklin D. Roosevelt made the monument a national park, increasing the level of protection afforded this wonder even more. The 62-mile coastal strip was added to the park in 1953.

The peninsula itself has a long history of boom-and-bust cycles. Cities on the northern coast jockeyed over the right to collect customs charges from incoming shipping, while other towns rose up overnight in anticipation of the transcontinental railroad.

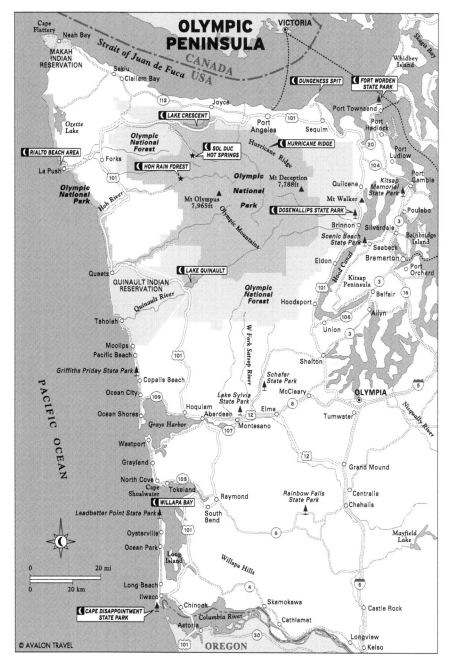

HIKING THE COAST

The Olympic coastline can be dangerous to hikers. Two "watch out" situations are attempting to round headlands and getting caught by incoming tides, and being struck by floating logs in the surf. Park Service offices have a helpful *Olympic Coastal Strip* handout with a map and dos and don'ts for backcountry users. Note that the Hoh and Quillayute Rivers are too deep to ford at any time, and that other creeks and rivers may be difficult to cross, particularly at high tide or when runoff is strong. Always take a tide chart and use caution. This is, after all, the wilderness.

Unfortunately for locals, in 1873 the railroad decided to end its route in Tacoma instead, dashing the region's hopes and sending it into decline. Still, the hardworking and genuine folks who live here have always found a way to survive.

Farther south at the mouth of the Columbia River, Washington's coast holds an important historical position as the landing point of Meriwether Lewis and William Clark at the end of their transcontinental journey in 1805; they had finally "reached the great Pacific Ocean which we been so long anxious to See." Because game proved scarce and the Washington side of the Columbia lacked protection from winter storms, they crossed the river to build a winter camp called Fort Clatsop near present-day Astoria, Oregon.

PLANNING YOUR VISIT

A ringed network of roads makes sightseeing easy here. Highway 101 follows three sides of the peninsula and joins Highways 8 and 12 to complete the loop. Visitors can continue their journey down Highway 101 past Willapa Bay all the way down to the Columbia River.

Trailheads within the Olympic National Forest require a **Northwest Forest Pass** (800/270-7504, www.fs.fed.us/r6/feedemo, $30 annual, $5 daily).

General Park Information

Olympic National Park is unique in that there are no roads running through its pristine land—the only way to visit the interior is to hike or ride horseback. The park is circled by the Highway 101 loop. A $15 park entrance fee, good for seven days, is charged for vehicles, or $5 for those on foot or bikes. A variety of annual and lifetime National Park passes are also available from the park service. Entrance fees are collected at Elwha, Hurricane Ridge/Heart O' the Hills, Hoh, Sol Duc, and Staircase entrance stations. Backcountry users should be sure to request a copy of the **Olympic Wilderness Trip Planner** from the Wilderness Information Center (360/565-3100, www.nps.gov/olym) in Port Angeles. **Wilderness use permits** ($5 for the permit, plus $2 pp/night) are required for backcountry camping; pick one up at the WIC or the ranger station nearest your point of departure. Because of overuse, summer quotas are in effect and reservations are required for overnight hikes in the Ozette, Flapjack Lakes, Hoh, Grand and Badger Valleys, Lake Constance, and Sol Duc areas.

CLIMATE

This area is has an undeniable mystical quality, right down to the most unusual weather. Peninsular weather is dominated by the Olympic rain shadow. Simply put, the Olympic mountain range causes the moist sea air to dump its precipitation before crossing the high peaks. That's why cities directly east of the mountains see 10–17 inches of rain per year, but the western slope of the mountain might see upwards of 160 inches! Three-quarters of the national park's precipitation falls October–March, and even during the relatively dry months, it's best to be ready for rain. The geography helps keep temperatures mild, generally ranging from the low 70s in summertime to the mid-40s in the winter.

Hood Canal and Vicinity

The Kitsap Peninsula is separated from the Olympic Peninsula by the Hood Canal, a 1.5-mile-wide, 65-mile-long channel of saltwater. Highway 101 follows the west side of the "Canal Zone," providing a delicious tidewater drive through second-growth forests with countless vistas of the waterway from every possible angle. The road hugs the canal, tucking in and out of various inlets along the way. Much of the route between Quilcene and Union is minimally developed, and scattered resort estates dot the shoreline. Several places sell freshly shucked oysters along the way. At the southwest corner of Hood Canal, the waterway makes a sharp bend, angling northward and nearly turning the Kitsap Peninsula into an island. South from this elbow is the largest town in the area, Shelton, and at the head of the canal is the fast-growing region around Belfair.

In addition to the glorious vistas along Hood Canal, you'll discover camping and hiking at two state parks and on nearby Olympic National Forest and Olympic National Park lands, plus outstanding scuba diving and fishing. Lake Cushman is a popular fishing and summer recreation spot, just east of the Staircase entrance to Olympic National Park, and the dam at the lake's southeast end produces some of Tacoma's electricity.

History

Like many other features in Washington, Hood Canal received its name from Capt. George Vancouver during his 1792 exploration of Puget Sound. He called it "Hood's Channel," after a British naval hero, Lord Hood, but a printer's error in Vancouver's report changed the word channel to canal. Hood Canal is *not* a canal, but actually a long, glacially carved fjord. The waters of Hood Canal are more susceptible to pollution than other parts of Puget Sound because of limited tidal flushing. Rapid

© ERICKA CHICKOWSKI

Hood Canal

development around the southern end of Hood Canal has led to increasing concerns over water pollution, and several beaches have been closed to shellfish gathering in recent years.

HOOD CANAL BRIDGE

Hood Canal is spanned at only one point along its entire length, by the 6,471-foot-long **Hood Canal Floating Bridge** that connects the Kitsap and Olympic Peninsulas near Port Gamble. The world's third-longest floating bridge (the longest over tidewater) was opened in 1961 and served the peninsulas well until February 13, 1979, when a violent storm with 100-mph gales broke off and sank nearly a mile of the western portion of the bridge. In a remarkable feat of driving, a trucker in his 18-wheeler backed the semi at almost full throttle off the bridge when it began to sink. To prevent another sinking, the center span of the rebuilt bridge is now opened when wind conditions are severe. You can cast a line for salmon or bottom fish from the fishing pontoon; there's a special anglers' parking lot at the Kitsap end of the bridge. Keep your eyes open for submarines; the Navy's Trident fleet often passes through en route to or from the Bangor submarine base. Just north of the bridge, **Salsbury Point County Park** has a boat launch and camping.

SHELTON

The peaceful blue-collar town of Shelton (pop. 9,000) occupies the head of Oakland Bay on the southwest toe of Puget Sound. It is both the Mason County seat and the only incorporated city in the county. Put on your plaid shirt and baseball cap to blend in. It's easy to see the importance of timber here: a sprawling yellow Simpson Timber Co. lumber and plywood mill dominates the town, and the surrounding land is filled with tree farms in varying stages of regrowth. Rayonier Research Center, where the chemistry and manufacture of pulp is studied, is also here, as is a maximum-security state prison. Downtown has wide streets and a friendly atmosphere, but up the hill you'll find homogenized America, with a McDonald's, Wal-Mart, and Super 8 Motel.

© KITSAP PENINSULA VISITOR & CONVENTION BUREAU/JEAN BOYLE

The Hood Canal Bridge is the longest floating bridge over saltwater.

Mason County is one of the nation's largest Christmas tree–producing areas; every year, over two million trees are shipped worldwide. Originally named Sheltonville, the town was founded in 1855 by David Shelton. Forestry and oystering were, and still are, the primary industries here, beginning in 1878 when the first shipment of highly prized Olympia oysters left Kamilche.

Sights

The **Mason County Historical Museum** (5th St. and Railroad Ave., 360/426-1020, noon–5 P.M. Tues.–Fri., noon–4 P.M. Sat., donations accepted), in the old library building, emphasizes the importance of logging in Shelton's history with displays on railroad logging, historical photos, and artifacts.

"Tollie," the locomotive in downtown Shelton between 2nd and 3rd on Railroad Ave., is a 96-ton Shay logging engine that saw most of the country in its heyday. Behind it sits a red caboose housing the visitors center. Downtown Shelton has a number of antique shops scattered along Railroad Avenue.

The **Bronze Works** (50 W. Fredson Rd., 360/427-3857 or 888/821-0372, www.nw-webessentials.com/bronzeworks, 8 A.M.–5 P.M. Mon.–Fri., 10 A.M.–6 P.M. Sat.) is a critical part of the Kimberly T. Gallery and Sculpture Garden. Located four miles south of town on Highway 101, this is the only bronze foundry in Washington. Visitors can tour the facility and view finished pieces in the gallery; bronze is poured most Thursdays. Classes and workshops are available.

Tour the Department of Wildlife's **Shelton Trout Hatchery** (Eells Hill Rd., approximately eight miles north of Shelton, 360/426-3669, 8 A.M.–5 P.M. daily). Continue up the road, turning right at the sign marking Denny Ahl Seed Orchard, and cross over the 440-foot-high **Steel Arch Bridge** that spans the Skokomish Gorge.

Entertainment and Events

Little Creek Casino (91 W. Hwy. 108, 360/427-7711 or 800/667-7711, www.little-creek-casino.com, 9 A.M.–4 A.M. Sun.–Thurs., 9 A.M.–5 A.M. Fri.–Sat.) deals blackjack, craps, and roulette and hosts frequent no-limit Hold éEm tournaments. Try the inexpensive buffet dining or the surprisingly good café.

Early June's **Mason County Forest Festival** (www.masoncountyforestfestival.com) includes parades, a carnival, musical entertainment, arts and crafts, and logging competition in such events as the Two-Man Double Buck, Speed Climb, Ax Throw, and the ever-popular Jack and Jill.

Mason County Fair (www.masoncounty-fair.com) is held the last weekend in July at the fairgrounds. Highlights include live entertainment and traditional county fair favorites such as 4-H exhibits and cake and preserve competitions.

Come back in September for The West Coast Oyster Shucking Championship and Seafood Festival, a.k.a. **OysterFest** (www.oysterfest.org). The main event is high-speed oyster shucking, and those shells will fly. Surrounding the competition are two days of wine-tasting, an oyster cook-off, food booths, art and boating exhibits, dancers, bands, and magicians.

The holiday season brings Santa to Shelton during the annual **Christmas Parade and Bazaar** (www.sheltonchamber.org), held the first weekend in December with a parade by land and by sea.

Sports and Recreation

Play a quick round of golf at **Lake Limerick Country Club** (790 E. Saint Andrews Dr., 360/426-6290, www.lakelimerick.com) a fir tree–lined nine-hole course playable year-round.

Cyclists can check out a relatively level nine miles of forested single-track just north of Shelton. The Lower South Fork Skokomish Trail can be reached by taking Highway 101 north of town, turning west on Skokomish Valley Road, taking Road 23 to the Brown Creek Campground and then following Forest Service Road 2394 for a bumpy quarter mile.

Shelton is a good place to enjoy some of

Mason County's better hunting. Deer, elk, grouse, turkey, goose, and duck are all legal within season. Or, if you've got the guts, come out and take down a fearsome bear. Regulations are many and can be found at the Washington Department of Fish and Wildlife (360/902-2464, www.wdfw.wa.gov).

You'll need a boat to get to tiny **Stretch Point State Park** (12 miles north of Shelton next to the town of Grapeview, www.parks. wa.gov), which has no camping, showers, toilets, or drinking water but has one of the best sandy beaches around Puget Sound. Grapeview itself has vineyards, a country store, marina, and a sometimes-open museum.

Accommodations

When it comes to chain motels in Shelton, **Super 8 Motel** (2943 N. View Cir., 360/426-1654 or 800/843-1991, www.super8.com, $55 s or $65 d) is it. The rooms aren't a disaster, but they aren't all that comfy either. Most guests—even non-gamblers—would be better served heading into Hoodsport or splurging a little and checking in to the ◖ Little Creek Casino Resort (91 W. Highway 108, 360/427-7711, www.little-creek-casino.com, $145–275 d), which offers very nice rooms for reasonable rates. There's a spa on-site, plus an indoor pool and the ever-popular buffet restaurant.

Food

A good place to start the day is **Pine Tree Restaurant** (102 S. 1st, 360/426-2604, 5 A.M.–8 P.M. daily) a family place with big breakfasts served all day, plus seafood and steak for dinner.

Owned by Taylor United and managed by Xinh Dwelley—a talented Vietnamese chef and former oyster-shucking champ— ◖ **Xinh's Clam & Oyster House** (221 W. Railroad Ave., 360/427-8709, 5–9 P.M. Tues.–Sat.) delivers such treats as hot and spicy seafood soup, oysters sautéed in black bean sauce, and grilled halibut.

If tasty affordable food beats out elegance as your chief concern, try **Suzan's Grill** (1927 Olympic Hwy. N, 360/432-8939, www.su-zansgrill.com, 8 A.M.–3 P.M. Sun.–Thurs., Fri.–Sat. 8 A.M.–9 P.M.). This family-owned eatery trumpets "Nothing from Cans at Suzan's."

You can wallow in nostalgia and a big beefy burger at the same time at the local **A&W Family Restaurant** (1729 Olympic Hwy N., 360/426-2002). The drive-in still offers its namesake root beer and classic curbside service.

Get produce at the **Shelton Farmers Market** (3rd St. between Cedar and Franklin, 360/427-8260, 9 A.M.–2 P.M. Sat. mid-May to late-Sept).

Information and Services

For maps and festival information, contact the **Shelton-Mason County Chamber of Commerce** (in the caboose on Railroad Ave., 360/426-2021 or 800/576-2021, www.shelton-chamber.org. 9 A.M.–6 P.M. Mon.–Fri., 9 A.M.–3 P.M. Sat.–Sun. June–Sept., 10 A.M.–5 P.M. Mon.–Fri. Oct.–May.).

Mason General Hospital (901 Mountain View Dr., 360/426-3102) is the nearest emergency room to Shelton. Hurt pets can be taken to Haigh Veterinary Hospital (81 S.E. Walker Park Rd., 360/426-1840) or Shelton Veterinary Hospital (104 E. J St., 360/426-2616).

Getting There

Mason County Transit (360/427-5033 or 800/374-3747) has free bus service throughout the county. All buses are kitted-out with bike racks. **Olympic Air** (360/426-1477, www.olyair.com, $250 per hour) offers scenic flights over the area.

UNION

The scattered settlement of Union occupies land near the "elbow" where Hood Inlet angles abruptly to the northeast. Summer and weekend homes crowd the highway, struggling to find their place among the relics of the past, such as the very picturesque **Dalby Waterwheel,** built in 1923 and still able to generate electricity if the need arose. A few miles west is the **Skokomish Indian Reservation,** near the intersection of Highways 101 and 106.

You can tell you're on the reservation by all the fireworks stands that line the highway. The tribal center houses a small museum with arts and crafts.

Sights and Recreation

Twanoh State Park (seven miles east of Union on Hwy. 106, 360/902-8608, www.parks. wa.gov) is a very popular spot for picnicking beneath tall trees, and swimming and water-skiing on relatively warm Hood Canal. The 182-acre park also has several miles of hiking trails along scenic Twanoh Creek, sturdy CCC-constructed structures from the 1930s, a tennis court, a concession stand with snacks and groceries, bathhouses, and camping in tent ($19) and RV ($26) sites with coin-operated showers.

The Skokomish Tribe operates the **Lucky Dog Casino** (19330 N. US Hwy. 101, 360/877-5656, 9 A.M.–midnight Sun.–Thurs., 9 A.M.–2 A.M. Fri.–Sat.), a smoke-free house featuring slots, blackjack, Pai Gow, and an amateur Texas Hold éEm league with free tournaments.

Practicalities

The guest rooms at Union's elegant **(Alderbrook Resort and Spa** (7101 E. Hwy. 106, 360/898-2200 or 800/622-9370, www.alderbrookinn.com, $190–420 s or d) are simply but beautifully decorated, many augmented by views of the Olympic mountains. Its spa offers traditional services plus unique treatments such as ancient Hawaiian lomilomi massage. The downstairs Restaurant at Alderbrook showcases local seafood, and the bar serves beer, wine, and cocktails.

Robin Hood Village (6780 E. Hwy. 106, 360/898-2163, $85–155 d) has seven cottages with hot tubs and kitchenettes. The smaller, older ones fit two people cozily, while the newer, larger ones are ideal for two couples. Also on-site is the **Robin Hood Pub** (6791 E. Hwy. 106, 360/898-4400, 5–9 P.M. Wed.–Sun.), which serves a full range of meals from a $12 burger and fries up to a $40 tenderloin. Great desserts, too. **Union Country Store** (5130 E. Hwy. 106, 360/898-2641) has a small deli.

Mason County Transit (360/427-5033 or 800/374-3747) provides free bus service throughout the county.

HOODSPORT AREA

The town of Hoodsport is the largest along the west side of Hood Canal and can provide most of your travel needs. This is the place to get Forest Service and Park Service information and to stock up on food before heading north. Hoodsport's lodgings cater to scuba divers, particularly small groups who come to explore the amazingly diverse creatures in the deep, clear waters just offshore. The lack of strong currents and minor tidal fluctuations help make this a good place for beginning divers. Visibility is best in the winter—to 50 feet—when fewer plankton are in the water. Other people come to water ski, sail, windsurf, or to catch shrimp, fish, and crabs. The **Hood Canal Hatchery** is right in town.

Five miles north from Hoodsport is the village of **Lilliwaup,** with a general store and motel, an RV park, and a pair of restaurants. The little burg of **Potlatch** is two miles south of Hoodsport on Highway 101.

Potlatch State Park

Enjoy camping, diving, clamming, crabbing, and fishing in Hood Canal at Potlatch State Park (three miles south of Hoodsport on Hwy. 101, 360/877-6947, www.parks.wa.gov). Have a picnic on the water, or explore the underwater park with scuba gear. The park is named for the feasts held by many Northwestern Indians, in which the exchanging of gifts was the primary focus. The campground ($17 for tents, $23 for RVs) is open year-round.

Hoodsport Winery

A small, family-run operation, Hoodsport Winery (23501 Hwy. 101, 360/877-9894 or 800/580-9894, www.hoodsport.com) produces wine from Puget Sound fruits and berries and is especially known for its rhubarb wine. It also has varietal grape wines, including a surprising cabernet sauvignon. The tasting room is open 10 A.M.–6 P.M. daily.

Entertainment and Events

The main summer event is **Celebrate Hoodsport Days,** with a street fair, food, kids' parade, and fireworks on the first full weekend of July.

August brings the annual **Hood Canal Salmon Derby** (360/790-6589, www.sschapterpsa.com/Derby_Page.htm), where $25 and some angling luck can win a $1,000 prize. Kids' events and a barbecue are all part of the fun.

Sports and Recreation

Rent dive gear, get air refills, and take classes from **Hood Sport 'N Dive** (24080 N. Hwy. 101, a mile north of Hoodsport, 360/877-6818, www.hoodsportndive.com) or **Mike's Dive Center** (38470 N. Hwy. 101, Lilliwaup, 360/877-5324, www.mikesbeachresort.com). Both places also rent dive kayaks and sea kayaks.

Practicalities

Glen-Ayr Canal Resort (25381 N. U.S. Hwy. 101, 360/877-9522 or 866/877-9522, www.glenayr.com), 1.5 miles north of Hoodsport, is the most elaborate and diverse local resort, with motel rooms for $85–95 s or d. The one-bedroom suites start at $150. A hot tub, recreation room, and marina round out the amenities here. Or park at one of 38 RV sites with full hookups for $33 per day.

Sunrise Motel and Resort (24520 Hwy. 100 on the north side of Hoodsport, 360/877-5301, www.hctc.com/~sunrise) is a favorite of scuba divers and has rooms for $59–69 d. A package including a dorm bed for two nights and three days and including free air tank refills is $60 per person. RV sites are $30 per night, and pets cost an extra $10.

The **Waterfront Resort** (in Potlatch, 360/877-9422, motel $99 s or d, cabin $138–179 up to 6) offers quite nice shore-view rooms, plus manufactured home–style cabins with kitchens. The resort also rents spaces to RV campers ($38–43 full hookups).

You can't visit the Hood Canal without feasting on some oysters. In Hoodsport, the place to do it is ◖ **The Tides** (27061 N. U.S. Hwy. 101, 360/877-8921), a family diner that serves up shellfish and smiles. Try the pan-fried oysters, its best dish.

Information and Services

Stop by the **Hood Canal Ranger Station** (360/877-5254, 8 A.M.–4:30 P.M. Mon.–Fri. year-round, plus 8 A.M.–4:30 P.M. Sat.–Sun. mid-May to mid-Sept.) in Hoodsport for Olympic National Forest and Olympic National Park information.

Mason General Hospital (901 Mountain View Dr., 360/426-3102) is the nearest emergency room to Hoodsport. Sick pets can be taken to Haigh Veterinary Hospital (81 S.E. Walker Park Rd., 360/426-1840) or Shelton Veterinary Hospital (104 E. J St., 360/426-2616) in nearby Shelton.

Getting There

Mason County Transit (360/427-5033 or 800/374-3747) has free bus service along Hood Canal and throughout the county.

LAKE CUSHMAN AREA

Lake Cushman was a popular resort area at the turn of the 20th century, offering fishing, hiking, and hunting. By the 1920s, the two lakeside resorts had shut down and the city of Tacoma built a dam on the Skokomish River. When completed, the dam increased the lake's size tenfold to 4,000 acres. Though private summer homes are springing up around the lake, the area still has a decidedly remote feel, thanks in part to its protected neighbor, Olympic National Park, about 10 miles up the road.

Sights and Recreation

A once-upon-a-time state park, **Camp Cushman** (7211 N. Lake Cushman Rd., 360/877-6770, $5 day-use fee) is now managed by a private company. This 500-acre plot of rugged forest, pristine shoreline, and shaded picnic areas draws in recreational enthusiasts of all stripes. Anglers love to vie for cutthroat, kokanee, and rainbow trout in the lake. Divers come to explore the sunken forest and an old resort that was here before the dam was built. Hikers enjoy the four miles of hiking trails, leading from lake's edge to deep woods. Others come to swim, water ski, and, in winter, cross-country ski.

Camp Cushman makes for a good base camp to explore the area. Follow Lake Cushman Rd. to a T intersection at road's end; go left and follow the lake's edge to 70-foot **Cushman Falls,** near the lake's northwest end, about 11 miles from Hoodsport. Or, turn right at the T, then turn left in another 1.5 miles onto Big Creek Road 2419 for six miles to **Big Creek Viewpoint** for a sweeping view to the east.

The **Mt. Ellinor Trail** leaves Road 2419 at the five-mile point; the trail heads up one mile for a view over Lake Cushman. Hiking trails lead into Olympic National Park from Staircase Trailhead at the head of Lake Cushman, providing a range of hiking options. The **Flapjacks Lake** area is accessed by hiking up the North Fork Skokomish Trail, and then turning up the four-mile side route to the lake. For longer hikes, you can continue up the North Fork Trail, which connects to others, providing a number of lengthy loop-trip options. A steep and challenging three-mile trail switchbacks from the campground to **Wagonwheel Lake,** gaining over 3,200 feet en route.

Golfers can enjoy the summer sunshine at the nine-hole, par 35 **Lake Cushman Golf Course** (210 West Fairway Dr, 360/877-5505, greens fees $31–33), four miles west of Hoodsport.

Practicalities

Cushman Lake Resort (4621 N. Lake Cushman Rd., 800/588-9630, www.lakecushman.com) has rustic cabins ($55–135 d) with kitchens and baths; canoe, personal watercraft, and boat rentals; a convenience store, plus tent and RV sites.

Camp in one of the two campgrounds at **Camp Cushman** (7211 N. Lake Cushman Rd., 360/877-6770, $20 tents, $26 RVs with hookups), with loads of nearby recreation opportunities.

The Forest Service's **Big Creek Campground** (877/444-6777, www.recreation.gov, $10, open May–Sept.) is nine miles up Highway 119. The road ends after a total of 16 miles at **Staircase Campground** (www.nps.gov/olym, $12, no reservations), just west of the lake below the Staircase Rapids of the North Fork of the Skokomish River. This beautiful Olympic National Park site has year-round camping surrounded by old growth forest. Chose a riverside site for the ultimate nighttime lullaby.

ELDON TO BRINNON

Not much to Eldon—just a café, gas station, shellfish farms, and a diver's resort. The Hamma Hamma River enters Hood Canal here, and a paved road leads to two Forest Service campgrounds on the edge of Olympic National Park. In the winter, bald eagles gather along the banks of the Hamma Hamma to feed on spawning salmon. Brinnon isn't much bigger than Eldon, but this stretch of Hood Canal has a number of interesting attractions.

Sights

C DOSEWALLIPS STATE PARK

A half mile south of Brinnon on Highway 101, Dosewallips State Park covers 425 acres at the base of the Olympic Mountains, offering both fresh- and saltwater activities where the Hood Canal comes together with the Dosewallips River. Enjoy camping ($17 for tents, $23 for RV hookups) and fishing for salmon and steelhead in the river. Clams are sometimes available here in season—check with the Washington Department of Fish and Wildlife (360/902-2700, www.wdwa.wa.gov). Six miles of hiking trails provide access to the forested west end of Dosewallips.

Two miles south of Brinnon, **Pleasant Harbor State Park** has a protected dock adjacent to a private marina, but no camping, boat launch, or swimming facilities.

HAMMA HAMMA RECREATION AREA

Hamma Hamma Road begins two miles north of Eldon and continues to the edge of the Mt. Skokomish Wilderness. **Hamma**

Hamma Campground (877/444-6777, www.recreation.gov, $10, May–mid-Nov.) is six miles up the road and can accommodate tents and trailers up to 22 feet in length. Continue another two miles to **Lena Creek Campground** (877/444-6777, www.recreation.gov, $10, year-round), which provides access to miles of hiking. **Lena Lake Campground** is a free walk-in campground at this pretty lake, a three-mile trek from the Lena Creek Campground. Expect a compost toilet and no potable water at this fairly primitive site. Built by the CCC in the 1930s, the historic **Hamma Hamma Cabin** (360/877-5254, $40) is available for groups up to six. This rustic abode has no running water.

Webb Lookout is a popular high spot, although it offers no Olympic views, just a broad shot of the canal. Take Hamma Hamma Road and turn right on a logging road at about 2.5 miles and follow the signs. Park along the road and hike the half-mile trail to the lookout.

MOUNT SKOKOMISH WILDERNESS
Covering a little more than 13,000 acres, the Mt. Skokomish Wilderness occupies steep terrain bordering the western edge of Olympic National Park. The **Putvin Trail** starts from Forest Road 25, approximately four miles beyond Lena Creek Campground on Hamma Hamma Road, and climbs steeply, rising more than 3,700 feet in less than four miles. The trail ends at rock-rimmed Lake of the Angels, just inside the park boundary. The Mt. Skokomish Wilderness is managed by Olympic National Forest (360/877-5254). Wilderness permits are not required.

DOSEWALLIPS RECREATION AREA
Scenic Dosewallips Road (Forest Road 2610) heads west from Brinnon, following the Dosewallips River into the heart of the Olympics and ending 15 miles later at Dosewallips Campground within Olympic National Park. Sadly, though, the road is washed out at mile 9.2 and may remain so for some time due to environmental concerns. Look for elk along the way. Approximately

three miles up is **Rocky Brook Falls.** The turnoff isn't marked, but look for the bridge and small hydro plant on the right side. It's a short walk to the 80-foot falls, but use care since water levels can change quickly.

The Forest Service's **Elkhorn Campground** (free, open May–Sept.) features sites right along the river approximately three-quarters of a mile past the washout on Dosewallips Road. Vault toilets are the rule here. **Dosewallips Falls** cascades over enormous boulders just inside the Olympic National Park boundary, about four miles past Elkhorn along the road-turned-trail. Just another mile farther is the National Park Service's **Dosewallips Campground** (www.nps.gov/olym, free, no reservations), a primitive site with no water and pit toilets. A trailhead here provides access to the park backcountry via the West Fork and Main Fork Dosewallips trails. The site is not to be confused with the easier-access Dosewallips State Park.

DUCKABUSH RECREATION AREA
Duckabush Road (Road 2519) heads west from Highway 101 four miles south of Brinnon, providing access to both the Brothers Wilderness and Olympic National Park. Four miles up Duckabush Road is the rustic **Interrorem Ranger Cabin,** built in 1907 as headquarters for Olympic National Forest. Today the Forest Service rents this historic four-person cabin for $30; call 360/877-5254 for details. Two short trails—the **Interrorem Nature Trail** and **Ranger Hole Trail**—provide access to the densely forested country near the cabin. Another mile up Duckabush Road is **Collins Campground** ($10, May–Sept.). Continue a short distance up Duckabush Road to Forest Road 2530, and follow it 1.3 miles. From here, **Marhut Falls Trail** climbs 0.75 mile to this picturesque waterfall.

BROTHERS WILDERNESS
This 16,682-acre wilderness lies within Olympic National Forest and occupies a blip of land on the eastern flank of Olympic National Park. Wilderness permits are not required in the Brothers Wilderness. Only a few developed

trails exist in the wilderness; the primary one is the **Duckabush River Trail,** which begins a mile up from the Collins Campground in Duckabush Recreation Area. The trail climbs six miles to the park boundary, with a view from Big Hump rock. Once inside the park, you can connect to a maze of other routes through the high country. From Lena Lake Campground on Hamma Hamma Road, a hiking trail leads uphill to Lena Lake on the edge of the wilderness, and then on to **Upper Lena Lake** inside Olympic National Park. This is a perfect overnight backcountry trip.

OTHER SIGHTS

In Brinnon, **Whitney Gardens & Nursery** (306264 Hwy. 101, 360/796-4411, www.whitneygardens.com, 9 A.M.–dusk daily, $1 admission, $2 for a guided tour) has seven acres of display gardens that include more than 3,000 rhododendrons, azaleas, and other flowering plants. It is especially stunning from mid-May to mid-June, but you'll find something in bloom all summer.

Learn how oysters, mussels, and clams are raised at Brinnon's **Point Whitney Shellfish Lab** (1000 Point Whitney Rd., 360/796-4601), run by the Washington Department of Fisheries.

In Eldon, the **Seafood Store** (38546 N. U.S. Hwy. 101, 360/877-5811 or 888/877-5844, www.hamahamaoysters.com) sells fresh shucked, smoked, shell, and even pickled oysters! Tours of the facility are welcomed.

Events

Brinnon's **Hood Canal ShrimpFest** (360/796-4886) over Memorial Day Weekend includes an art fair, street dance, boat show, farmers market, and shrimp cooking contests. Bring along your decorated belt sander to participate in the zany Belt Sander Race.

Recreation

A number of public campgrounds are described under *Sights.* In addition to these, the Forest Service's **Seal Rock Campground** ($12, open May–Sept.) is just north of Brinnon and fea-

tures saltwater-facing sites with great clam harvesting, as well as piped water and flush toilets. **Cove RV Park** (303075 U.S. Hwy. 101, 360/796-4723, $27 nightly, $170 weekly) has RV hookups, plus bathrooms and showers. It is located three miles north of Brinnon.

Accommodations

◖ **Mike's Beach Resort** (38470 Hwy. 101, Lilliwaup, 360/877-5324 or 800/231-5324, www.mikesbeachresort.com, $20 per person hostel, $70–130 d) is a fun and friendly place with a variety of accommodations, including dorm beds in a hostel with a full kitchen, cabins, and even Airstream RVs for rent. Tent spaces ($25) and RV hookups ($30) are also available, and pets are welcome throughout the resort. The main attraction here is the boat launch and dive facility; divers can fill tanks at the air station here, and for a fee even non-guests can launch boats or access the water from Mike's beach. There's great scuba diving at an artificial reef just offshore; ask about the eight-foot octopus.

Bayshore Motel (31503 Hwy. 101, 360/796-4220 or 800/488-4230, $55 s or d) has large and comfortable rooms.

Houseboats for Two (360/796-3440 or 800/966-5942, www.houseboats4two.com, $195–240 d) rents private one-bed houseboats afloat on Pleasant Harbor near Brinnon. The accommodations are luxurious and include a hot tub, fireplace, and pool. This is a favorite honeymoon spot.

Elk Meadows B&B (3485 Dosewallips Rd., 360/796-4886, www.elkmeadowswa.com, $95 d, no kids under 14) is a big ranch-style home three miles up Dosewallips Road in the heart of elk country. Two guest suites have private baths, and a full breakfast is served each morning.

Food

Brinnon's **Half Way House Restaurant** (41 Brinnon Lane at Hwy. 101, 360/796-4715, 7 A.M.–8 P.M. Sun.–Thurs., 7 A.M.–9 P.M. Fri.–Sat.) has a gourmet chef and reasonable prices on seafood, steak, burgers, and lighter fare.

This is also the place to go for a homemade breakfast. The **Geoduck Tavern** (307103 U.S. Hwy. 101, Brinnon, 360/796-4430, kitchen open 4–8 P.M. Tues.–Thurs., 11 A.M.–9 P.M. Fri.–Sat.) is a great place to soak up the local vibe. It serves up burgers and sometimes there's live music on weekends.

Getting There

Jefferson Transit (360/345-4777 or 800/833-6388, www.jeffersontransit.com) has bus service connecting Brinnon with Port Townsend, Sequim, and Poulsbo. **Mason Transit** (360/427-5033 or 800/374-3747) has free bus service south to Shelton and other parts of Mason County.

QUILCENE AREA

Tiny Quilcene has a rough-at-the-edges country feeling reminiscent of Northern California. The compact town has simple homes and trailers, piles of split wood in the yards, and smoke curling from the chimneys. Chainsaw carving is considered high art, and the surrounding cutover landscape looks like a bad haircut.

Sights

BUCKHORN WILDERNESS

Covering 44,258 acres, the Buckhorn Wilderness occupies barren ridges and peaks topping 7,000 feet within Olympic National Forest and bordering on the extensive wilderness within Olympic National Park. The **Mt. Townsend Trail** begins from Forest Road 2760 off Road 27, northwest of Quilcene. This six-mile route climbs to the top of 6,280-foot Mt. Townsend, providing incredible vistas in all directions. **Big Quilcene Trail** starts at the three-sided shelter 10 miles up Forest Road 2750 from Quilcene and follows the Big Quilcene River into the high country before switchbacking to the summit of Marmot Pass at 6,000 feet. From here, you can continue into Olympic National Park via the Constance Pass Trail. The Big Quilcene is famous for the multitudes of rhododendrons that bloom here in early summer. Contact the Hood Canal Ranger District (360/765-2200) for more information on the Buckhorn Wilderness.

MOUNT WALKER

The most popular viewpoint along Hood Canal is 2,804-foot **Mt. Walker,** five miles south of Quilcene. A narrow gravel road leads to the summit, or you can hike up via a two-mile path through tall Douglas fir forests and a lush understory of huckleberry and rhododendron. The trail (or road) emerges onto a ridge with panoramic views of Seattle, Mt. Rainier, and the Cascades to the east, and the Olympics to the northwest. Bring a lunch to enjoy at the summit picnic area.

OTHER SIGHTS

Two miles south is the **Quilcene National Fish Hatchery** (360/765-3334, open daily, hours vary). The **Quilcene Historical Museum** (360/765-4848, noon–5 P.M. Fri.–Mon. late Apr.–late Sept.) houses a historic kitchen, old logging and farming tools, and a millinery exhibit.

Events

The **Olympic Music Festival** (360/732-4800, www.olympicmusicfestival.org) is a summertime concert series held weekends late June to early September in a century-old barn located 10 miles west of Hood Canal Bridge, off Highway 104. Donkeys wander the grounds as patrons sit on hay bales in the barn listening to chamber music or enjoy picnics outside with mountain (and cow) vistas. The Philadelphia String Quartet and guest artists perform these "Concerts in the Barn" 0.25 mile south of Highway 104 on Center Road.

Recreation

The Forest Service's very popular **Falls View Campground** (877/444-6777, www.recreation.gov, $10; open May–Sept.) is 3.5 miles south of Quilcene and offers 14 RV sites without hookups and 16 tent sites. The half-mile **Falls View Canyon Trail** drops down to the Big Quilcene River from the campground. Additional campsites can be found at **Lake Leland Park** (six miles north of Quilcene, $12, open Apr.–Oct.), a small county facility that has a boat ramp for small boats and a dock, plus a short nature trail.

Accommodations and Food

Enjoy the wooded scenery at Quilcene's **Mount Walker Inn** (360/765-3410, www.mountwalkerinn.com, $65–95 s or d), a humble little place with rooms featuring kitchenettes. No telephones in rooms, but pets and kids are welcome.

Prime rib, roast beef, and seafood (including ultra-fresh local oysters) distinguish the **Timber House** restaurant (295534 U.S. Hwy. 101, 360/765-3500, 11 A.M.–9 P.M. Mon.–Fri., 9 A.M.–9 P.M. Sat.–Sun.), a half mile south of Quilcene.

Information

The Olympic National Forest **Quilcene Office of the Hood Canal Ranger District** (295142 Hwy. 101, 360/765-2200) has maps and information on local camping and hiking options on both Forest Service and National Park lands.

Port Townsend

Standing on the northern tip of Quimper Peninsula—a point off the northeast corner of the Olympic Peninsula—Port Townsend (pop. 9,000) is best known for its many excellent Victorian homes. Sandwiched between the perpetually snow-covered Olympic Mountains and the ship-filled Strait of Juan de Fuca, Port Townsend is a working town with much to see and explore. Many folks consider it one of the most interesting and beautiful towns in Washington.

History

Port Townsend is the main port of entry to Puget Sound and the first town site on the Olympic Peninsula. As such, the city has hosted consulates from Chile, Sweden, Norway, Germany, France, Great Britain, and the kingdom of Hawaii. The hopes that the port city would be the end point for the Union Pacific's transcontinental railroad fueled a huge late-1800s building boom, resulting in the grand Victorian mansions still in evidence today. A period of financial depression followed, and many of the mansions were abandoned and converted into rooming houses and apartments, left to wait forlornly for the rescue that would eventually save a small percentage of these historical beauties.

Over the years, military bases and a pulp and paper mill restored Port Townsend's economic stability. The "far-out" location attracted a hippie crowd in the 1970s, leaving an indelible mark on the city's culture. Today tourism, fed by a gorgeous setting with breathtaking views over Admiralty Inlet and the nearby Olympic Mountains, accounts for much of Port Townsend's prosperity. Many of the remaining Victorian mansions have been transformed into lavish B&Bs, and several galleries, shops, and gourmet restaurants have sprung up to serve visitors from near and far. Today the citizens of Port Townsend are a blend of blue-collar millworkers, generally harmless tree-huggers, and wealthy newcomers and retirees.

SIGHTS

Port Townsend's main attractions are its historic late 19th-century homes and businesses, along with impressive Fort Worden State Park. Downtown's main boulevard, Water St., consists of stout brick buildings filled with fine galleries, restaurants, and shops selling antiques, books, clothing, wines, and gifts.

One of the more distinctive town sights is the **Haller Fountain,** which features a bronze, scantily clad maiden emerging from a shell that is supported by water-spraying cherubs and fish. Theodore N. Haller donated the fountain to the city "in memory of early pioneers."

Port Townsend is still very much a seafaring town. Its Port Hudson Harbor is jammed with yachts, and quite a few boatbuilding businesses are based nearby. Of particular note is the **Northwest School of Wooden**

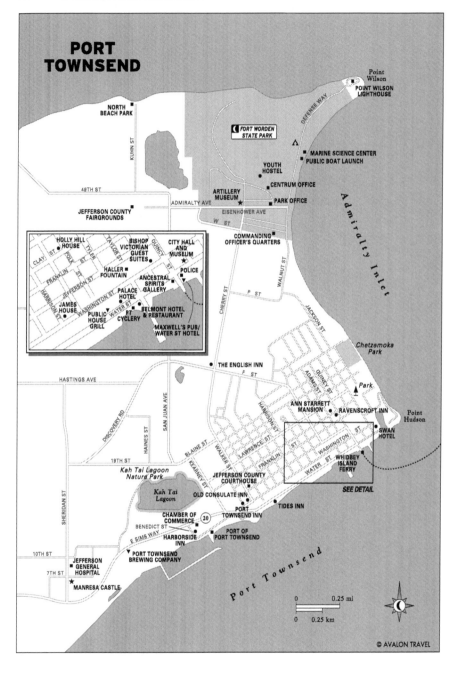

PORT TOWNSEND

Point Wilson
POINT WILSON LIGHTHOUSE

NORTH BEACH PARK

DEFENSE WAY

KUHN ST

FORT WORDEN STATE PARK

MARINE SCIENCE CENTER
PUBLIC BOAT LAUNCH

YOUTH HOSTEL

49TH ST

CENTRUM OFFICE

ARTILLERY MUSEUM
PARK OFFICE

ADMIRALTY AVE

JEFFERSON COUNTY FAIRGROUNDS

EISENHOWER AVE

W ST

COMMANDING OFFICER'S QUARTERS

Admiralty Inlet

HOLLY HILL HOUSE

BISHOP VICTORIAN GUEST SUITES

CITY HALL AND MUSEUM

CLAY ST
TYLER ST
POLK ST
TAYLOR ST
QUINCY ST

HALLER FOUNTAIN

POLICE

FRANKLIN ST

ANCESTRAL SPIRITS GALLERY

JEFFERSON ST
HARRISON ST
WASHINGTON ST
WATER ST

PALACE HOTEL

JAMES HOUSE

PUBLIC HOUSE GRILL

PT CYCLERY

BELMONT HOTEL & RESTAURANT

MAXWELL'S PUB/ WATER ST HOTEL

WALNUT ST

CHERRY ST

P ST

JACKSON ST

Chetzemoka Park

THE ENGLISH INN

HASTINGS AVE

F ST

QUINCY ST
ADAMS ST

Park

DISCOVERY RD

HAINES ST

SAN JUAN AVE

HARRISON ST

ANN STARRETT MANSION

RAVENSCROFT INN

Point Hudson

BLAINE ST

LAWRENCE ST

ST

WASHINGTON ST

SWAN HOTEL

19TH ST

WALKER ST
KEARNEY ST

FRANKLIN ST

WATER ST

WHIDBEY ISLAND FERRY

Kah Tai Lagoon Nature Park

JEFFERSON COUNTY COURTHOUSE

SEE DETAIL

Kah Tai Lagoon

OLD CONSULATE INN

SHERIDAN ST

CHAMBER OF COMMERCE

20

PORT TOWNSEND INN

TIDES INN

BENEDICT ST

E SIMS WAY

HARBORSIDE INN

PORT OF PORT TOWNSEND

10TH ST

PORT TOWNSEND BREWING COMPANY

JEFFERSON GENERAL HOSPITAL

7TH ST

MANRESA CASTLE

Port Townsend

0   0.25 mi

0   0.25 km

© AVALON TRAVEL

Boatbuilding (42 N. Water St., 360/385-4948, www.nwboatschool.org, 10 A.M.–4 P.M. Mon.–Fri.), where several-day classes and six- and nine-month programs develop skills through intensive classes and hands-on projects. The facility is also open for self-guided tours.

Historic Tours

Stop by the chamber of commerce (2437 E. Sims Way, 360/385-2722, www.ptchamber.org) to pick up a tour map of historic downtown and other parts of Port Townsend. Guided tours of the waterfront, saloons, and historic homes are available by appointment from **Kathy Hill Step On Tours** (360/385-4356, $10).

Historic Home Tours are held the third weekend in September; owners of private Victorian residences open their doors to the public. Call the visitor information center for tickets (360/437-4065, $16).

Uptown

A second section of historic Port Townsend, "Uptown," covers a block or so of Lawrence Street near Taylor Street. This is where you're more likely to meet people who actually live in town. It was created as a turn-of-the-20th-century shopping district for the genteel ladies living in the hilltop mansions, a place to avoid the bawdy waterfront shopping district ("the most wicked city north of San Francisco" in the 1880s). Today, Uptown's mansions are elaborate B&Bs and offbeat stores. You'll discover great views across Admiralty Inlet from a tiny park at Monroe and Clay Streets.

Museums

Housed in the city's 1891 City Hall Complex, **Jefferson County Historical Society Museum** (210 Madison St., 360/385-1003, www.jchsmuseum.org, 11 A.M.–4 P.M. daily, $4 adults, or $1 children 3–12), this excellent museum rambles over three floors of boat exhibits and models, intricate baskets, button and bottle collections, a Victorian

bedroom, and even two buffalo-horn and bearskin chairs from an old photo studio. Downstairs is the old city jail, in use until the 1940s.

There's also a small museum inside the lobby of the **post office** (1322 Washington St.). During the 1880s, this imposing stone building served as the Customs House, the port of entry for all international traffic into Puget Sound.

Another building of interest is the **Jefferson County Courthouse,** standing high on a hill at Jefferson and Walker Streets. Built in 1892, this redbrick building is one of Washington's oldest courthouses and is notable for the 100-foot-tall clock tower that serves as a beacon to mariners.

Rothschild House

The Rothschild House (Franklin and Taylor St., 11 A.M.–4 P.M. daily Apr.–Oct., 10 A.M.–5 P.M. Sat.–Sun. Nov., closed Dec.–Mar., $4 adults, $1 children 3–12) was built in 1868 by D. C. H. Rothschild, a Port Townsend merchant and a distant relative of Germany's famous Rothschild banking family. This restrained Victorian still has much of the original furniture, wallpaper, and carpeting, and it is surrounded by herb and flower gardens.

Manresa Castle

The Manresa Castle (651 Cleveland St., 360/385-5750 or 800/732-1281, www.manresacastle.com, free) is an 1892 mansion variously owned by a tycoon, the Jesuit Order, and a hotelier. Originally, Manresa had only one bathroom per floor, but when the film *An Officer and a Gentleman* was filmed, the Hollywood crew ran out of rooms at other hotels and motels. Their contracts called for a bathroom for each room, so the studio made a deal with Manresa's owner: It advanced him money against the rent, and it was used to build the 43 bathrooms of today. A restaurant and lounge are on the premises, and an attractive rose and rhododendron garden provides a quiet place to enjoy the vista of Port Townsend and Admiralty Inlet.

Ann Starrett Mansion

Easily the most opulent Victorian structure in Port Townsend, the Ann Starrett Mansion (744 Clay St., 360/385-3205 or 800/321-0644, www.starrettmansion.com, noon–3 P.M. daily, $2 adults, kids under 12 free) is a National Historic Landmark and a favorite B&B. Take a tour or stay here to enjoy the luxury up close. The rooms are furnished with period antiques and offer outstanding views. Dormer windows in the dome admit light that illuminates a different red ruby stone for each season of the year.

Old Fort Townsend State Park

Old Fort Townsend State Park (4 mi. south of town, 360/385-3595) has campsites and seven miles of hiking trails through tall firs, sloping down to a 150-foot cliff along Port Townsend Bay. The 377-acre park is open mid-April to mid-September only. A fort was established here in 1856 to guard against possible American Indian attacks. The fort was used during World War II as an enemy munitions defusing station. In 1958 it was turned over to the State Parks Commission. A short self-guided historical walk starts at the display board near the park entrance.

◖ Fort Worden State Park

Capping Point Wilson, Fort Worden, along with Fort Flagler on Marrowstone Island and Fort Casey on Whidbey Island, served as the "Iron Triangle" of forts protecting the entrance to Puget Sound. Fort Worden's guns were never fired in battle, and advances in military technology made them obsolete almost as soon as they were in place. After the army left in 1953, Fort Worden served as a state detention center before becoming a state park in 1973. If the place seems familiar, it may be because much of the movie *An Officer and a Gentleman* was filmed here.

Many of the fort's buildings remain, the highlight being the **Commanding Officer's House** (10 A.M.–5 P.M. daily June–Aug., noon–4 P.M. Sat.–Sun. Mar.–May and Sept.–Oct.,

one weekend per month Nov.–Feb., $2 adults, $1 kids 6–12, free for kids under 6) containing period Victorian furnishings. One of the old barracks buildings now houses the **Coast Artillery Museum** (360/385-0373, 10 A.M.–5 P.M. daily July–Aug., 11 A.M.–4 P.M. daily the rest of the year, $2 adults, $1 kids 6–12, free for kids under 6), where you'll learn how the enormous gun batteries out on the coastal bluffs worked.

Don't miss the photo op provided by the 1917 **Point Wilson Lighthouse.** No public tours of the building are offered, but the beach here makes for wonderful sunup or sundown strolls, with dramatic Mt. Baker seeming to rise directly across the water.

Contemporary facilities include a campground, boat launch, tennis courts, underwater scuba-diving park, rhododendron garden, hiking trails, and a hostel. Also visit the **Port Townsend Marine Science Center** (360/385-5582, www.ptmsc.org, hours and days vary by exhibit, $5 adults, $3 kids 6–17, free for kids under 6, discounts Nov.–Mar.) offering intimate, hands-on relationships with local sea creatures, beach walks, and evening slide shows and lectures.

ENTERTAINMENT AND EVENTS
Live Music

The Public House Grill & Ales (1038 Water St., 360/385-9708, www.thepublichouse.com, 11 A.M.–11 P.M. daily) has live music on in-season weekends, and good pub food, especially for lunch. **Ajax Café** (21 N. Water St., Port Hadlock, 360/385-3450, www.ajaxcafe.com, 5–9 P.M. Tues.–Sun.) also has live music most weekend nights.

Theater

Rose Theatre (385 Taylor St., 360/385-1089, www.rosetheatre.com) is a refurbished and reinvigorated old-time movie house, now showing concerts, plays, and the occasional art-house movie. The **Key City Public Theatre** puts on plays and musicals throughout the year at the Key City Playhouse (419 Washington St.,

360/385-7396, www.keycitypublictheatre.org). The **Port Townsend Community Orchestra** (360/732-6898, www.porttownsendorchestra.org) gives four free performances between October and May.

Events

Port Townsend's calendar is jam-packed with activities, many of which are sponsored by the nonprofit **Centrum Foundation** (360/385-3102 or 800/733-3608, www.centrum.org). These include events such as performances by jazz, bluegrass, blues, and classical musicians; folk dance festivals; plays; seminars; and readings by well-known authors. For a schedule of upcoming events, contact the Centrum Foundation.

Held the third week in May, the **Rhododendron Festival** (www.rhodyfestival.org) features a big Saturday parade, dances, antique and art shows, a carnival, rhododendron displays, and the pomp and circumstance of choosing rhododendron royalty.

The summertime music season kicks off with the **Festival of American Fiddle Tunes** (360/385-3102 x127, www.centrum.org) at the end of June, followed by mid-July's **Jazz Port Townsend**, which blends directly into the **Port Townsend Blues Festival** (360/385-3102 X127, www.centrum.org).

The second weekend in August is reserved for the **Jefferson County Fair,** (www.jeffcofairgrounds.com), the old-fashioned kind with livestock shows, 4-H displays, and a mud race. A particular highlight of the year's calendar is the **Wooden Boat Festival** (www.woodenboat.org) in early September, full of music, regattas, boat tours, and exhibitions.

Early October brings the fairly strange **Kinetic Sculpture Race** (www.ptkineticrace.org) to Port Townsend; costumed characters pilot human-powered mechanical sculptures over land *and water* in a race to the finish.

If you're in town on the first Saturday in December, you'll be able to join the fun as Santa arrives by ferry, and people gather to sing carols on Water Street and watch the **tree lighting ceremony** (360/385-7911).

SHOPPING

Water Street houses numerous art galleries, antique shops, cafés, trendy gift shops, and an import toy store. **Ancestral Spirits Gallery** (921 Washington St., 360/385-0078, www.ancestralspirits.com, 10 A.M.–6 P.M. Sun.–Fri., 10 A.M.–8 P.M. Sat.) features an impressive blend of modern and traditional Native American art, masks, and jewelry. **Earthenworks Gallery** (1002 Water St., 360/385-0328, www.earthenworksgallery.com, 10 A.M.–5:30 P.M. daily) sells high quality, creative works—especially ceramics. **Gallery Walks** are held the first Saturday of each month, 5:30–8 P.M. March–Dec., during which galleries hang new works, serve refreshments, and often have artists on hand. Walks are self-guided, so just show up downtown and go for a walk!

FairWinds Winery (1984 Hastings Ave. W., 360/385-6899, www.fairwindswinery.com, noon–5 P.M. daily Memorial Day–Labor Day) is a tiny family operation producing mainstream varietals as well as some unique offerings such as Aligote and its award-winning Fireweed Mead.

RECREATION
City Parks

Chetzemoka Park on Admiralty Inlet at Jackson and Roosevelt Streets is a small, shady park with eight flower gardens, picnicking, a bandstand, and beach access. Bird-watchers may be interested in **Kah Tai Lagoon Nature Park** (12th St. near Sims Way), which encompasses 85 acres of wetlands, grasslands, and woodlands, explorable through 2.5 miles of trails.

Water Sports

PT Outdoors (Flagship Landing on Water St., 360/379-3608, www.ptoutdoors.com) has kayak lessons, rentals, and tours. A kayak with paddles and life vest will run you $45 for a half day's use. The 133-foot, 1913 schooner *Adventuress* (360/379-0438, www.soundexp.org) sails on voyages of all lengths throughout the summer and fall. Rates range from a

$40 day cruise up to $400 for a three-night San Juans cruise. The ship allows no smoking nor alcohol, and all meals are vegetarian. **Brisa Charters** (360/376-3264, www.olympus.net/brisa_charters, $75 per person) offers day and sunset sails about the 45-foot Lapworth sloop, the *Annie Too*.

South of Port Townsend, **Anderson Lake State Park** (Anderson Lake Rd. and Hwy. 20) is an isolated lake surrounded by trees. No camping or swimming, but it's a popular place to fish for cutthroat and rainbow trout, although toxic algae blooms in the lake have limited its use in the last few years.

Camping
Fort Worden State Park (360/385-4730, www.parks.wa.gov, $33–38 full hookups, $19–21 tent, $7 extra reservation fee) has 50 year-round beachside campsites and another 30 near the conference area. All of these sites accommodate RVs with full hookups. A mere five primitive tent sites are available, as are coin-op showers.

Four miles south of town, **Old Fort Townsend State Park** (360/385-3595, www.parks.wa.gov, $17) has shady campsites under tall firs along Port Townsend Bay. It also has showers. The campground is open for camping mid-April to mid-September only.

RVers can park at the private **Point Hudson Resort** on the beach (360/385-2828 or 800/826-3854, $35 full hookups) or the campground adjacent to the **Jefferson County Fairgrounds** (4907 Landes St., 360/385-1013, www.jeffcofairgrounds.com/camping.htm, $20).

Other Recreation
PT Outdoors (Flagship Landing on Water St., 360/379-3608, www.ptoutdoors.com) rents basic cruising bikes for $15 per half day or $25 for the full day. For mountain, touring, and tandem bikes rental, check **P.T. Cyclery** (252 Tyler St., 360/385-6470, www.ptcyclery.com) The store has created several maps of great mountain-bike rides in the area, for bikers looking for places to hit the trails. You can also

rent bikes, sea kayaks, and camping gear from **Sport Townsend** (1044 Water St., 360/379-9711, www.sporttownsend.com)

Peninsula Sportsman (360/379-0906, www.peninsulasportsman.com) outfits and guides a wide variety of family or individual expeditions, from salmon, trout, or halibut fishing to trophy hunting for sea ducks.

Port Townsend Athletic Club (229 Monroe St., 360/385-6560) has exercise and weight rooms, racquetball courts, yoga and cardio classes, and a sauna and hot tub.

Local golf courses include the public eighteen-hole **Discovery Bay Golf Club** (7401 Cape George Rd., 360/385-0704, www.discobaygolf.com, $28 weekdays, $32 weekends). The **Port Townsend Golf Club** (1948 Blaine St., 360/385-4547, www.porttownsendgolf.com, $16 nine holes, $23 eighteen holes) is a municipal par-35, said to be the driest course on the Olympic Peninsula.

ACCOMMODATIONS
Port Townsend has some of the most exquisite lodging choices in the state, most notably the myriad old Victorian homes that have been turned into bed-and-breakfasts, along with a dozen or so motels and hotels, and an equal number of cabins and guesthouses. The city is a popular destination, and reservations are advised, especially in the summer and on weekends. The chamber of commerce (360/385-2722, www.ptchamber.org) tracks local accommodations and can tell you where rooms are available.

Under $100
Enjoy daily all-you-can-eat pancake breakfasts at the uniquely placed ◖ **Olympic Port Townsend AYH Hostel** (360/385-0655, www.hiayh.org, $17 dorm beds, $45 couples' rooms), located in a former barracks building at Fort Worden. Reservations are strongly advised in summer months, especially for the couples' rooms. The hostel is open year-round, but guests must be out 9:30 A.M.–5 P.M.

For a bit of a step up—and more privacy—try **Port Townsend Inn** (2020 E. Washington

St., 360/385-2211 or 800/216-4985, www. porttownsendinn.com, $68 s or d). The normal rooms are pretty standard hotel fare with unremarkable furniture, but the grassy grounds are nice and there's an indoor pool and hot tub on the premises. Splurgers can upgrade to a whirlpool-bath suite ($168 d) with wet bar.

Built in 1885, the **Belmont Hotel and Restaurant** (925 Water St., 360/385-3007, www.thebelmontpt.com, $79–129 s or d), was once host to sailors, ship captains, and gamblers. The ornately decorated Italianate-style inn right in the heart of downtown offers guests a chance to savor the past.

The Waterstreet Hotel (635 Water St., 360/385-5467 or 800/735-9810, www.waterstreethotelporttownsend.com, $50–160 s or d) is on the second and third floors of the 1889 N. D. Hill Building, with Water Street Brewing and Ale House on the first level. Suites with private decks overlooking the bay are available.

Built in 1889, the **Palace Hotel** (1004 Water St., 360/385-0773 or 800/962-0741, www.palacehotelpt.com, $59–159 s or d), once the "Palace of Sweets" brothel, is a beautifully restored boutique hotel with antique furnishings, high ceilings, and old-world charm. Rooms come decorated with antique furnishings and high ceilings, some with shared and some with private baths. Continental breakfast is served daily.

$100-150

For a piece of Hollywood history, stay at **Tides Inn** (1807 Water St., 360/385-0595 or 800/822-8696, www.tides-inn.com, $68–269 s or d), where parts of the 1982 film *An Officer and a Gentleman* were filmed. Some rooms have private decks and hot tubs and some have kitchenettes; a newlywed suite is also available.

Harborside Inn (330 Benedict St., 360/385-7909 or 800/942-5960, www.harborside-inn.com, $90–160 s or d) is a 63-room waterfront motel with large rooms (each with a microwave, fridge, a private patio, and a striking view), an outdoor pool, hot tub, and continental breakfast.

A charming, three-tier wedding-cake Victorian house at the end of Water St. near Admiralty Inlet is home to **The Swan Hotel** (222 Monroe St., 360/385-1718 or 800/776-1718, www.theswanhotel.com). The property offers romantic little studio cottages ($160 d), suites ($99–145 d), and one penthouse unit ($275–400 d). The lodging is friendly to kids and dogs, even both at the same time.

Six miles west of Port Townsend on a bluff overlooking Discovery Bay is **Bay Cottages** (4346 S. Discovery Rd., 360/385-2035, www.baycottagegetaway.com, $85–150 s or d). The property's two cottages each include full kitchen, feather beds, and fresh flowers. Kids are welcome.

Holly Hill House (611 Polk St., 360/385-5619 or 800/435-1454, www.hollyhillhouse.com, $108–190 s or d), built in 1872, has been beautifully renovated to provide five guest rooms, each with a private bath. The parlor showcases the owner's collection of military aviation artwork and WWII memorabilia. The home is surrounded by tall holly and elm trees.

Standing on a hill, with a garden, gazebo, and outdoor hot tub on the patio, **The English Inn** (9718 F St., 360/385-5302 or 800/254-5302, www.english-inn.com, $99–135 s or d) is a lush, tastefully decorated inn. All five guest rooms have British themes and small private baths.

$150-200

One of Port Townsend's most remarkable bed-and-breakfast inns sits inside **◖ Manresa Castle** (651 Cleveland St., 360/385-5750 or 800/732-1281, www.manresacastle.com, $109–229 s or d), a unique 1892 castle-hotel with antique furnishings and bay views. Each room is unique, with one-of-a-kind antique furnishings and lavish linens. A spacious tower room set within the castle's turret is a favorite among honeymooners.

Explore the private English gardens and then settle into the comfortable rooms at **Bishop Victorian Guest Suites** (714 Washington St., 360/385-6122 or 800/824-4738, www.bishopvictorian.com, $135–225 s or d). Rooms feature period decorations, Victorian lighting, fireplaces, and kitchenettes. A continental breakfast is included.

Ann Starrett Mansion (744 Clay St., 360/385-3205 or 800/321-0644, www.starrettmansion.com) has nine rooms ($115–175 s or d) in the 1889 mansion and two in a separate cottage ($179–225 s or d). A gourmet breakfast is served.

Stay in a lovely turreted Queen Anne at ◖ **The Old Consulate Inn** (313 Walker St., 360/385-6753 or 800/300-6753, www.oldconsulateinn.com, $99–210 s or d), overlooking Port Townsend from atop a high bluff. Once the office of the German Consul, this 1889 beauty has fireplaces in two parlors, a large billiard and game room, and playable grand piano and antique organ. A gazebo encloses the hot tub. Eight guest rooms all have private baths. A gourmet breakfast is served.

Three short blocks from downtown, the elegant **Ravenscroft Inn** (533 Quincy St., 360/385-2784 or 800/782-2691, www.ravenscroftinn.com, $109–210 s or d) features wide verandas with sound and mountain views in a custom-built B&B. The eight guest rooms have private baths, and two suites have fireplaces and tubs. Elegant gourmet breakfasts will get you out of bed, guaranteed.

James House (1238 Washington St., 360/385-1238 or 800/385-1238, www.jameshouse.com, $145–210 s or d) is known for the dizzyingly elegant decor of its antique-laden guest rooms. Most offer commanding views of the town, as well as private baths and a relaxing garden that looks out on the water. There's also a secluded bungalow with two beds ($250 d).

$200-250

An interesting alternative lodging—especially for families and groups—is one of the former officers' homes in **Fort Worden State Park** (360/344-4400). The 32 houses have mostly been refitted with Victorian-style furnishings and modern conveniences. These cozy homes sleep 7–14 guests. Rates begin at $104 per night for a one-bedroom apartment unit and go up to $375 for an 11-bedroom barracks. Because of their popularity—especially during summer festivals—reservations for these houses should be made far in advance.

FOOD
Cafés and Diners

The Wild Coho (1044 Lawrence St., 360/379-1030, www.thewildcoho.com, 5–10 P.M. Thurs.–Sun.) is an Uptown eatery serving an eclectic breakfast, lunch, and dinner menu of vegetarian specials, black-bean chili, frittatas, and fruit blasts.

Salal Café (634 Water St., 360/385-6532, 7 A.M.–2 P.M. daily) has a lovely sundeck and a wide variety of fresh breakfast and lunch options. Come here to enjoy the homemade jams and famous potatoes and salsa.

Lehani's (221 Taylor, 360/385-3961, 7 A.M.–6 P.M. daily) is another downtown spot for morning coffee and baked goods, delicious chocolate treats, and quick lunches.

Stop by **Sea J's Café** (2501 Washington St., 360/385-6312, 6 A.M.–8 P.M. Mon.–Sat., 7 A.M.–8 P.M. Sun.) for the best fish and chips in town.

Great sub sandwiches to go can be found at **Jordini's** (924 Washington St., 360/385-2037, 11 A.M.–7 P.M. daily).

Contemporary Northwest

Sandwiched between a launderette and a Radio Shack store, ◖ **T's Restaurant** (2330 Washington St., 360/385-0700, www.ts-restaurant.com, 4–10 P.M. Wed.–Mon., closed Tues., entrées $20–31) is a big surprise. Step inside to find an elegant atmosphere and Italian-inspired Northwest seafood and meats.

Fountain Café (920 Washington St., 360/385-1364, 11:30 A.M.–3 P.M. and 5–9 P.M. daily) serves wide-ranging gourmet dishes full of local ingredients and fresh seafood in its small but charming backstreet location. It's a popular place, so be ready to wait for a table on summer weekends.

◖ **Silverwater Café** (Washington and Taylor Streets, 360/385-6448, 5–9 P.M. daily, entrées $10–15) is well known for fresh and reasonably priced pasta, meat, and seafood served in a bright and airy space.

International

Lanza's Ristorante/Pizzeria (1020 Lawrence St., 360/379-1900, 5–9 P.M. daily) in Uptown has several kinds of excellent pizzas, plus outstanding home-cookin' in the form of antipasto and pastas. A simpler but nevertheless tasty choice is to get a slice of pie and a Coke at **Waterfront Pizza** (951 Water St., 360/385-6629, 11 A.M.–8 P.M. daily). It's the perfect place to try a sourdough-crust pizza if you've never had one before.

Ichikawa and Sushi Bar (1208 Water St., 360/379-4000, 11 A.M.–1:30 P.M. and 5–9 P.M. Tues.–Sat., closed Sun.–Mon.) serves up sushi, sashimi, and robata-yaki, as well as grilled and alder-smoked seafood, chicken, and steaks.

Pub Grub

Port Townsend Brewing Company (330 10th St., 360/385-9967, www.porttownsendbrewing.com) brews a variety of quality beers, including a pale ale, stout, IPA, and a bitter. You can check out the different flavors in the tasting room.

For the full sit-down brewpub experience, check out **Waterstreet** (126 Quincy St., 360/379-6438, noon–10 P.M. daily) with very tasty pub food like steamed mussels, oyster shooters, hearty burgers and grilled sandwiches, plus several home-brewed beers to wash them down.

Markets

Located in Uptown, **Aldrich's Grocery** (940 Lawrence St., 360/385-0500, 7 A.M.–9 P.M. daily) has all the staples, but you'll also find gourmet specialties and a big wine selection. The deli here (Sally's) makes fantastic baked goods and the best soups around.

Find fresh fish and other seafood at **Key City Fish Co.** (307 10th St., 360/379-5516 or 800/617-3474, www.keycityfish.com, 9 A.M.–6 P.M. Mon.–Sat., closed Sun.), right next to the ferry terminal. They'll pack your fish in ice to take home aboard the ferry.

Get baked goods, organic produce, crafts, and flowers at the **Port Townsend Farmers Market** (360/379-5054) held downtown 8:30 A.M.–1 P.M. Saturday May–October and in Uptown 3:30–6 P.M. Wednesday May–August.

INFORMATION AND SERVICES

For local information and a ton of brochures, head to the **Port Townsend Chamber of Commerce Tourist Information Center** (2437 E. Sims Way, 360/385-2722 or 888/365-6978, 9 A.M.–5 P.M. Mon.–Fri., 10 A.M.–4 P.M. Sat., and 11 A.M.–4 P.M. Sun.). For general tourist information about the town, look up www.ptguide.com on the Web.

Port Townsend Public Library (1220 Lawrence St., 360/385-3181) is one of the many Carnegie Libraries built early in this century.

The local emergency room is at Jefferson Healthcare Emergency (834 Sheridan St., 360/385-5600). Sick pets can find help at Chimacum Valley Veterinary Hospital in nearby Port Haddock (820 Chimacum Rd., 360/385-4488).

GETTING THERE
By Car and Bus

Parking can be a nightmare on summer weekends; avoid the hassles (and parking tickets) by parking at the Park & Ride (Haines Pl. and 12th St.); stop on the south side of town and hop aboard a **Jefferson Transit** (360/385-4777 or 800/773-7788, www.jeffersontransit.com) bus, serving Port Townsend and Jefferson County.

By Ferry

Port Townsend is served directly by the **Washington State Ferry** (206/842-2345 or 888/808-7977, 800/843-3779 for automated information, www.wsdot.wa.gov/ferries/) from Keystone on the southwest side of Whidbey Island. The ferries depart about every 50 minutes, and in summer cost $2.60 one-way for passengers and walk-ons, $11.15 one-way for car and driver, $0.50 extra for bikes.

P.S. Express (360/385-5288, www.puget-soundexpress.com, $78 round-trip, bikes and kayaks $12 extra) provides passenger-only service between Port Townsend and Friday Harbor on San Juan Island. The boat leaves Port Townsend daily April–October and takes you through Admiralty Inlet and the Strait of Juan de Fuca, where you're likely to see seals, sea otters, and orcas. The boat stays in Friday Harbor long enough for a quick three-hour visit, or you can overnight there and return to Port Townsend later.

By Air
Goodwin Aviation (360/531-1727) offers charter service to Sea-Tac Airport, Victoria, the San Juan Islands, and other Northwest destinations.

Oak Bay Area

Those who chose to motor up to Port Townsend from the Kitsap Peninsula or the rest of the Hood Canal area would do well to take the slow route up along the gentle waters of Oak Bay on Oak Bay Road. The stretch from the Hood Canal Bridge all the way to Port Townsend will have you pass little villages such as Port Ludlow, Port Hadlock, and Irondale, as well as the pastoral Marrowstone Island. Each of these has a cluster of businesses and a number of fascinating historic homes, including **Hadlock Manor** on Curtiss Street in Hadlock, built in the 1890s by a Swedish sea captain.

SIGHTS
Shine Tidelands State Park
Shine Tidelands State Park (www.parks. wa.gov) occupies a 13-acre spot at the north end of the Hood Canal Bridge and is popular with sea kayakers and windsurfers. No camping is allowed.

Fort Flagler State Park
Marrowstone Island's biggest attraction is Fort Flagler State Park, at the island's northern tip. Surrounded by water on three sides, the park is perfect for boating, picnicking, crabbing, and fishing. Wooded hiking trails and camping at beach sites are also available in this 783-acre park. Since it is in the Olympic rain shadow, the park gets lots of sun and only 17 inches of rain per year.

Fort Flagler joined with Fort Worden and Whidbey's Fort Casey to guard the narrow Admiralty Inlet against hostile incursions into Puget Sound. Built in the late 1890s, the fort served as a training center during the two World Wars. The massive gun emplacements were, thankfully, never needed for anything but gunnery practice. The fort was closed in 1955 and later became a state park. Today, nine gun batteries remain. From these, you can watch the ships, barges, sailboats, and fishing vessels cruise past; it's pretty easy to see why a fort was built on this strategic bottleneck.

Fort Flagler's spacious green parade grounds are bordered by barracks and gracious old officers' quarters. Several trails cut through wooded sections of the park. The **Marrowstone Point Lighthouse** (closed to the public) stands on the northeast edge of the fort, with massive Mt. Baker creating an attractive photographic backdrop.

Other Marrowstone Island Sights
Quiet Marrowstone Island is off the beaten path but offers wooded country, attractive summer homes, and a fascinating historic fort. The only real business on the island is **Nordland General Store,** which rents sea kayaks.

Upper Oak Bay Jefferson County Park on the southwest corner of Marrowstone Island has fine views east across Puget Sound. Summer-only camping is available, but no hookups or showers.

Tiny, boat-friendly **Mystery Bay State Park** (www.parks.wa.gov), just north of

COASTAL DEFENSE FORTS

A trip down the Pacific Coast of Washington is bound to reveal an interesting piece of the state's military heritage. Nestled among the bluffs and sandy beaches is a series of concrete bunkers that once protected the shore against enemy assault. The network runs along the entire coast, especially focused at the mouth of the Puget Sound and the Columbia River delta. These massive guns never drew a bead on a hostile force, but the picturesque ruins now make a great spot for a picnic.

In the North Puget Sound, the military history buff can check out what was once known as the **Iron Triangle,** the zone formed by Fort Casey, Fort Flagler, and Fort Warden, meant to protect the Puget Sound's cities as well as the strategically important Bremerton shipyard. What are now **Fort Casey State Park** on Whidbey Island, **Fort Flagler State Park** on Marrowstone Island, and **Fort Warden State Park** near Port Townsend all make for excellent historical hikes, and the elevated views of Admiralty Inlet are stunners at each park. The true artillery fan should focus on Fort Casey with its two salvaged 10-inch disappearing carriage guns and two three-inch AA emplacements.

Fort Ebey, on the eastern shore of Whidbey Island near Coupeville, has a gorgeous view, and the grassy field makes an excellent rest stop for a Whidbey Island bike ride. It's not as impressive from a historical perspective – it only housed two six-inch guns, and today nothing is left but earthworks and concrete. Likewise for Camp Hayden near Port Angeles, now part of the Salt Creek Recreation Area: Once home to a 16-inch naval cannon and a six-inch disappearing carriage gun as well as 150 soldiers, today nothing is left but a damp concrete bunker, some rusting metal, and one heck of a nice campground.

Guarding the strategic chokepoint at the entrance to the Columbia River is **Fort Canby,** an outpost established in 1852. This battery was used sporadically for training up until 1947. None of the six-inch long-range guns remain today, but the mossy concrete structures at what is now Cape Disappointment State Park are fascinating to roam.

Nearby **Fort Columbia** is one of the few intact defense emplacements along the coast, meaning that virtually all barracks, officers' quarters, and battery buildings are still there and available for exploration. Two decommissioned six-inch guns are also viewable at this site, although they were purchased from Canada in 1994, obviously not part of the fort's original armament.

Nordland, has a picnic area, beach, pier, boat moorage, and protected waters for small boats, along with striking Olympic views, but no camping.

PRACTICALITIES
Port Ludlow

The Inn at Port Ludlow (1 Heron Rd., 360/437-2222 or 800/732-1239, www.portludlowresort.com, $109 d–$599 for 8) dominates Port Ludlow. Port Ludlow offers the utmost in luxury: large heated outdoor and indoor pools, hot tub, saunas, squash and tennis courts, paved bike paths, three nine-hole golf courses, and 300-slip marina on Port Ludlow Bay complete with rental sailboats. A wide variety of rooms are available, from standard rooms to four-bedroom suites that sleep eight.

Harbormaster Restaurant in the Resort at Port Ludlow (1 Heron Rd., 360/437-7400, 7:30 A.M.–2 P.M. Sun.–Wed., 7:30 A.M.–10 P.M. Thurs.–Sat.) serves breakfast, lunch, and dinner, with entertainment most nights in the lounge. The outside deck is a favorite place for a romantic evening meal.

The **Port Ludlow Farmers Market** (360/437-0882) comes to town 9 A.M.–2 P.M. Fridays May–early September.

Port Hadlock

A 1911 plant built to distill alcohol from sawdust has found new life as the swanky **[** **Inn at**

Port Hadlock (310 Hadlock Bay Rd., 360/385-7030 or 800/785-7030, www.innatporthadlock.com). Just east of Port Hadlock on the way to Indian and Marrowstone Islands, this most unusual lodge and restaurant counts an in-house art gallery among its amenities. Hotel rooms go for $189–299 d. The reasonable steak and seafood restaurant provides fine harbor views and has a popular Sunday brunch.

Ferino's Pizzeria (846 Ness Corner Rd., 360/385-0840, 11:30 A.M.–8 P.M. Mon.–Thurs., 11:30 A.M.–9 P.M. Fri.–Sat., 3–8 P.M. Sun.) bakes outstanding gourmet pizzas and sells them by the slice. Also in Port Hadlock is **Ajax Café** (271 Water St., 360/385-3450, 11 A.M.–9 P.M. daily) with the best steaks in the area, plus a variety of creative Northwest seafood and chicken dishes. There is live music on weekends.

Chimacum Café (9253 Rhody Dr., Chimacum, 360/732-4631, 6 A.M.–9 P.M. daily in summer, 6 A.M.–8 P.M. daily rest of year) another locals' favorite, makes all-American steaks, chicken, burgers, and chocolate malts.

Marrowstone Island

The Ecologic Place (10 Beach Dr., 360/385-3077 or 800/871-3077, www.ecologicplace.com, $85–160 d) in Nordland has 11 rustic cabins with Oak Bay and Olympic views. Each comes with complete kitchen and bath facilities, plus a woodstove. There's a two-night minimum; no pets allowed.

The best bet on Marrowstone is at **Fort Flagler State Park** (360/902-8600 or 888/226-7688, www.parks.wa.gov). Three of the fort's old buildings are rented out as vacation homes ($105–170) and the campground ($14 tents, $20 full hookups, $7 extra reservation fee, late Feb.–Oct.) accommodates tenters and RV campers. Coin-operated showers are available.

INFORMATION

Stop at the **Olympic Peninsula Gateway Visitor Information Center** (Hwy. 104 and Beaver Valley Rd., Port Ludlow, 360/437-0120, 9 A.M.–4 P.M. daily in summer) for local information and brochures.

GETTING THERE

Jefferson Transit (360/385-4777 or 800/773-7788, www.jeffersontransit.com) serves all of Jefferson County, with connections to Port Angeles via Clallam Transit or the Kitsap Peninsula via Kitsap Transit.

Sequim

As storms pass over the Olympic Peninsula, they split in two; one part clings to the Olympics and the other is blown along by the strait's air currents, bypassing Sequim (pronounced SKWIM) like an island in the stream. The result is Sequim's famous "blue hole"—a miraculous gap in the sky of cerulean cloudlessness. The 17 inches of rain that fall here are less than fall on Los Angeles, and a typical year has 299 days of sun. The pleasant climate has transformed this former farming and mill town into a booming retirement community, with more than 25,000 people spread across the surrounding Dungeness Valley.

SIGHTS

Museum and Arts Center

One block north of Highway 101 lies the Museum and Arts Center (175 W. Cedar St., 360/683-8110, www.sequimmuseum.org, 9 A.M.–4 P.M. Mon.–Sat., 1–4 P.M. Sun., donation requested). Built to store the 12,000-year-old tusks, bones, and artifacts unearthed at Sequim's famous Manis Mastodon Site, the museum has branched out to include several antique cedar bark baskets, pioneer farming displays, and timber exhibits.

◖ Dungeness Spit

The word Dungeness (meaning sandy cape)

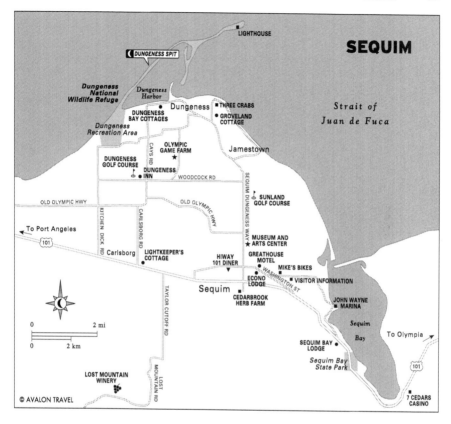

is a fitting description for this 5.5-mile-long stretch of sand that creates Dungeness Bay. The **Dungeness National Wildlife Refuge** (Voice of America Rd., 360/457-8451, www. fws.gov/washingtonmaritime/dungeness, $3 per group) provides habitat for 250 species of birds on the nation's longest natural sand spit. As many as 30,000 birds rest at this saltwater lagoon during their migratory journeys.

Built in 1857, the **New Dungeness Lighthouse** at the tip of the spit is managed by volunteers and offers tours, but you'll have to hike a total of 10 miles round-trip to see it. It's a good idea to check the tide charts before starting out. For an overview of the area, hike the half-mile trail from the parking lot to a bluff overlooking Dungeness Bay.

Clamming, fishing, and canoeing are permitted in this protected wildlife refuge, but no camping, dogs, firearms, or fires. The spit is closed to horses on weekends and holidays April 15–October 15.

Wineries

Two local wineries produce wines from eastern Washington grapes. **Olympic Cellars** (255410 Hwy. 101, 360/452-0160, www. olympiccellars.com, 9:30 A.M.–5:30 P.M. daily) is housed in a century-old cedar barn along Highway 101 just west of Sequim. The three women who run the place, known collectively as "The Olympic Women in Wine," produce wines under their Working Girl, La Dolce Vida, and Dungeness labels.

Lost Mountain Winery (3174 Lost Mountain Rd., 360/683-5229, www.lost-mountain.com, 11 A.M.–5 P.M. daily in summer, Sat.–Sun. only the rest of the year) makes robust, Italian-style red wines with no added sulfites.

Olympic Game Farm

The **Olympic Game Farm** (1423 Ward Rd., 360/683-4295 or 800/778-4295, www.olygamefarm.com, 9 A.M.–dusk daily, $10 adults, $8 seniors and ages 6–12, free for kids under 6), a vacation and retirement home for Hollywood's animal stars, is a 90-acre preserve where Gentle Ben and over 200 other animals of TV and movie fame can be visited. Many of the Walt Disney nature specials were filmed here, along with parts of many feature movies. Hour-long guided walking tours are available daily mid-May to early September. The park is open all year for driving tours for the same prices. Follow the signs from Sequim five miles northwest to Ward Road.

Farm Tours

Dungeness Valley's mild climate is perfect for growing herbs, and it is now one of only two places in the world where lavender oil is produced (the other is France). Many farms grow lavender locally; visit www.lavendergrowers.org for more information. Gourmet cooks will enjoy a visit to Washington's first herb farm, **Cedarbrook Herb Farm** (986 Sequim Ave. S, 360/683-7733, www.lavenderfarms.com/cedarbrook, 10 A.M.–5 P.M. Mon.–Sat., noon–5 P.M. Sun.), where 200 varieties of herbs, teas, and flowers are organically grown.

Other Sights

If you appreciate the unusual, drop by **Troll Haven** (360/797-7168, www.trollhaven.org) in Gardiner. This private residence is chock-full of sculptures and artwork depicting Scandinavian fairy-tale creatures. There are even live bison! Get here by heading east from Sequim on Highway 101 to Gardiner, and turning onto Gardiner Beach Road. Please respect the privacy of the landowners while

© ERICKA CHICKOWSKI

Lavender farms scatter the country roads in Sequim.

viewing the art from a distance, or call in advance to request a tour.

John Wayne loved the Northwest because he could visit the area and not be hounded by autograph seekers, and he especially loved the Strait of Juan de Fuca. The Duke liked it so much he bought land on Sequim Bay and donated it for a marina. The **John Wayne Marina** has 422 slips, a landscaped park and picnic area, and a bronze statue of the Duke as he appeared in the 1949 flick *She Wore A Yellow Ribbon*. Rent boats here at **The Bosun's Locker** (360/683-6521, www.portofpa.com/marinas/john-wayne-marina.html, 9 A.M.–6 P.M. daily). Bosun's also sells John Wayne souvenirs.

The enormous **7 Cedars Casino** (270756 Hwy. 101, 360/683-7777 or 800/458-2597, www.7cedars casino.com), near Blyn at the head of Sequim Bay, has bingo, blackjack, craps, keno, poker, and roulette; it is run by the Jamestown S'Klallam Tribe. Inside, several restaurants serve a variety of cuisines from regional favorites to hot dogs and fries. Also here is **Northwest Native Expressions Gallery** (360/681-4640, 9 A.M.–5 P.M. daily), with masks, paintings, jewelry, and weaving.

The artist's co-op **Blue Whole Gallery** (129 W. Washington St., 360/681-6033, bluewholegallery.com, 10 A.M.–5 P.M. Mon.–Sat., 11 A.M.–3 P.M. Sun.) features pieces by local artists.

EVENTS

Maybe a festival celebrating ditch-digging doesn't excite you. But the **Sequim Irrigation Festival** (www.irrigationfestival.com) is the longest-running festival in Washington State, so it must have something going for it! Parades, art and flower shows, a carnival, fireworks, logging show, and a one-of-a-kind chainsaw carving contest (second largest in America!) commemorate the annual event, held on the first full week of May each year.

In July, the **Celebrate Lavender Festival** (877/681-3035, www.lavenderfestival.com) features tours of local lavender farms, speakers, and an open-air market offering food, music, and demonstrations.

SPORTS AND RECREATION
Camping

Dungeness Recreation Area (554 Voice of America West, 360/683-5847), a 216-acre Clallam County park at the base of the refuge, has camping February–October ($18) with showers, beach access, and a picnic area. **Sequim Bay State Park** (just east of Sequim on Hwy. 101, 888/226-7688, www.parks.wa.gov, $19 tent, $24 full hookups, $7 extra reservation fee) offers wooded tent sites, RV hookup sites, a boat launch, scuba diving, hiking, tennis courts, and superb views of Sequim Bay.

The Forest Service offers campgrounds in the mountains 11 miles south of Sequim via Forest Roads 2909 and 2958 at **Dungeness Forks Campground** ($10, open late May–early Sept.). This well-water and vault-toilet hideaway has 10 sites close to hiking and fishing. Trailers and motor homes might have a tough time on the road. Contact the Quilcene Ranger Station (360/765-3368) for details.

Sequim's best RV park is **Rainbow's End RV Park** (261831 Hwy. 101, 360/683-3863, $34 daily, $193 weekly), where you can catch rainbow and golden trout in the property's stocked fishing pond. This pet-friendly park offers a fenced off-leash area, laundry and shower facilities, and free wireless Internet. There's a creek bordering the property and plenty of views of the mountains.

Other Recreation

Recreation in the Sequim area focuses on the protected waters inside the inner harbor of Dungeness Bay, a favorite place for windsurfers and sea kayakers. The six-mile path to the lighthouse on Dungeness Spit is a very popular place for a seaside walk or horseback ride. **Dungeness Kayaking** (360/681-4190, $90 per person, minimum of two) leads beginners on sea kayak trips around the bay.

Mountain bike rentals and tours of the nearby foothills are available from **Mike's Bikes** (551 W. Washington St., 360/681-3868, www.mikes-bikes.net, 10 A.M.–6 P.M. Mon.–Fri., 10 A.M.–5 P.M. Sat., closed Sun.).

One superb full-day ride near Sequim is up Forest Road 2860, which winds up the side of the Dungeness River Valley (with spectacular views) to a junction with the end of the Lower Dungeness Trail. The 11-mile single-track descent to Gold Creek is one of the best on the Olympic Peninsula, if not the entire state. Get there by car via Palo Alto Road, which leaves Highway 101 three miles east of Sequim, following signs to Forest Road 28. The lazy can arrange for a lift up the dirt road, but the downhill ride just isn't quite as satisfying that way.

The **Sequim Aquatic Recreation Center** (610 N. 5th Ave., 360/683-3344, www.sarcfitness.com) has two swimming pools, a gym, racquetball courts, exercise equipment, and a sauna.

Northwest golfers will be in heaven in Sequim, where it is possible to play a round just about any month of the year. There are several championship courses within city limits, but the best is unquestionably the par-72 **Dungeness Golf Course** (north of Carlsborg on Woodcock Rd., 360/683-6344, www.dungenessgolf.com, greens fees $34–39 for 18 holes in summer), which keeps greens pristine and poses some good challenges with its well-positioned bunkers. It's also got a pretty decent 19th hole: the Dungeness Inn Restaurant.

ACCOMMODATIONS

The Sequim Chamber of Commerce's website (www.visitsun.com) has links to most local motels and B&Bs in the area.

Under $100

Greathouse Motel (740 E. Washington St./Hwy. 101 E, 360/683-7272 or 800/475-7272, $45–79 s or d) includes a continental breakfast in the nightly rates. **Sequim West Inn** (740 W. Washington St., 360/683-4144 or 800/528-4527, www.sequimwestinn.com, $52–99 s or d) has rooms with microwaves and fridges.

Similarly, **Econo Lodge** (801 E. Washington St., 360/683-7113 or 800/488-7113, $79 s or $85 d) offers rooms with microwaves and fridges, plus a continental breakfast.

$100-150

Privacy seekers will love the **Lightkeeper's Cottage** (206 Carlsborg Rd., 360/681-2055, $125 d), a self-contained one-bedroom cottage with a full kitchen on a secluded, quiet property just west of Sequim. **Sequim Bay Lodge** (1788 Hwy. 101 E, 360/683-0691 or 800/622-0691, www.sequimbaylodge.com, $90–150 s or d), three miles east of town, has an outdoor pool and hot tub. **Dungeness Bay Cottages** (140 Marine Dr., 360/683-3013 or 888/683-3013, www.dungenessbay.com, $120–170 d) is five miles north of town along the bay and has five cottages with full kitchens on a private beach.

East of Sequim, find **Sunset Marine Resort** (40 Buzzard Ridge Rd., Blyn, 360/681-4166, www.sunsetmarineresort.com, $125–215 d), where generally pet-friendly six-person cabins with kitchens are spread over cliffs and grassy shorelines. **Groveland Cottage** (4861 Sequim-Dungeness Way, 360/683-3565 or 800/879-8859, www.grovelandcottage.com, $110–155 s or d) is a century-old house with a large lawn and pond five miles north of Sequim. Inside are five whimsical guest rooms with private or shared baths.

$150-200

Located across from the marina, **Sequim Bay Resort** (2634 West Sequim Bay Rd., 360/681-3853, www.sequimbayresort.com, $130–200 s or d) offers waterfront views from its lightly wooded property. The grounds are scattered with seaside cabins—some with kitchenettes—and campsites.

Just north of the main town are the **Juan de Fuca Cottages** (182 Marine Dr., 360/683-4433 or 866/683-4433, www.juandefuca.com, $155–305 s or d), six fully equipped housekeeping cottages perched on a 50-foot cliff overlooking Dungeness Spit. A hot tub is available. There is a two-night minimum on weekends.

Flower fans won't want to miss the gardens at ❖ BJ's Garden Café B&B (397 Monterra Dr., Port Angeles, six miles north of Sequim, 360/452-2322 or 800/880-1332, www.bjgarden.com, $160–240), a Victorian-style B&B

with award-winning greenery that's been featured in national magazines such as *Country Garden*. Each of the five guest rooms comes with fireplaces; some have jetted tubs.

$200-250

Colette's B&B (339 Finn Hall Rd., 360/457-9197, www.colettes.com, $195–395 s or d) is a luxurious 10-acre seaside estate with flower gardens, whirlpool baths, king-size beds, fireplaces, and gourmet breakfasts.

FOOD

Start out the day at **Oak Table Café** (292 W. Bell, 360/683-2179, 7 A.M.–3 P.M. daily) where the breakfasts are filling and delicious (try the wonderful soufflé-style baked apple pancakes).

Housed in a historic white church, **Jean's Deli** (134 S. 2nd Ave., 360/683-6727, 7 A.M.–3 P.M. Mon.–Fri. year-round, also 10:30 A.M.–3 P.M. Sat. in summer) is the best lunch spot in town, with delightful pastries, sandwiches, and espresso.

◖ The Three Crabs (Three Crabs Rd., 360/683-4264, 11:30 A.M.–7 P.M. Sun.–Thurs., 11:30 A.M.–8 P.M. Fri.–Sat.) has served Dungeness crab and other local seafood specialties for nearly 30 years at its waterfront location. It also has a retail seafood market. The crabs are well prepared, but the rest of the rather pricey menu isn't noteworthy.

Another place for fast and well-prepared lunches is **Hiway 101 Diner** (392 W. Washington St., 360/683-3388, 6 A.M.–8 P.M. Mon.–Thurs., 6 A.M.–9 P.M. Fri.–Sat., 7 A.M.–8 P.M. Sun.) a "fabulous fifties" family diner with the biggest local burgers. It's also popular for breakfast.

The **Dungeness Inn** (491-A Woodcock Rd., 360/683-3331, 4–9 P.M. Mon.–Fri., 9 A.M.–9 P.M. Sat.–Sun.) overlooking the Dungeness Golf Course, specializes in prime rib, steak, and seafood. **Tarcisio's** (609 W. Washington St., 360/683-5809, 7 A.M.–8 P.M. Sun.–Thurs., 7 A.M.–9 P.M. Fri.–Sat.) is the place to go for from-scratch pizzas.

Fans of Mexican food will enjoy two local eateries: **Las Palomas** (1085 E. Washington, 360/681-3842, 11 A.M.–9 P.M. daily) and **El Cazador** (531 W. Washington, 360/683-4788, 11 A.M.–9 P.M. Sun.–Thurs., 11 A.M.–10 P.M. Fri.–Sat.). The latter has a pleasant outside deck.

The **Sequim Open Aire Market** (2nd and Cedar, 360/683-9523) takes place 9 A.M.–3 P.M. Saturday late May to mid-October.

INFORMATION

For maps, brochures, and lots of local information drop by the helpful **Sequim-Dungeness Valley Chamber of Commerce Visitor Information Center** (1192 E. Washington St., 360/683-6690 or 800/737-8462, www.visitsun.com, 9 A.M.–5 P.M. daily).

GETTING THERE

Clallam Transit (360/452-4511 or 800/858-3747, www.clallamtransit.com) connects Sequim with Port Angeles, Forks, and Neah Bay. **Jefferson Transit** (360/385-4777, www.jeffersontransit.com) has transportation east to Port Townsend and Poulsbo.

Olympic Bus Lines (360/417-0700 or 800/457-4492, www.olympicbuslines.com, $49 one-way) has a daily shuttle to Sea-Tac Airport.

Port Angeles

Port Angeles is the largest city on the northern Olympic Peninsula and the gateway to many of its pleasures. Its busy harbor, protected by the strong sandy arm of Ediz Hook, is visited daily by logging ships, fishing boats, and the Victoria ferry MV *Coho*. The view from the Port Angeles city pier is breathtaking: Rocky Hurricane Ridge, made more ominous by a wispy cloud cover, seems to rise straight out of the turbulent waters of the Strait of Juan de Fuca. Because of its location as an entry point to both Vancouver Island (via the ferry) and to nearby Olympic National Park, Port Angeles bustles during the summer.

History

The original inhabitants along the northern shore of the Olympic Peninsula—members of the S'Klallam, Hoh, Quinault, Quileute, and Makah tribes—lived off the bounty of the land and waters, establishing fishing camps along the sandy beaches. Although the area was mapped by Spain in the late 18th century, whites did not permanently settle here until 1857. The town did not truly blossom until 1862, when a customs inspector named Victor Smith decided that Port Angeles should take over customs duties from already-established Port Townsend. This did not sit well with the residents of Port Townsend, but the dispatch of a warship to their harbor helped bring them around to the idea. That same year, President Abraham Lincoln named large sections of Port Angeles and Ediz Hook military reservations. The township of Port Angeles was thusly laid out by the federal government. The Board of Trade was moved to call it the "second National City"— second, that is, to Washington DC.

Like many seaside locations, Port Angeles once struggled with being so close to the tideline. In 1914, a massive engineering project sought to raise the level of local streets using walls and pilings, leaving many former first-stories beneath the level of the new sidewalk. The resulting "underground" is still visible in places around town.

Summer anchorage of parts of the U.S. Navy's Pacific Fleet through the 1920s and '30s helped sustain the local economy in those tough times. Long a major lumber and fishing town, Port Angeles became more reliant on tourism after the 1997 closing of the big Rayonier pulp mill and the declining salmon runs. Port Angelinos hope that feeding, sheltering, and entertaining many of the three million visitors that visit the Olympic National Park each year will help to pick up the slack.

SIGHTS
Municipal Pier and Marine Laboratory

The best part of Port Angeles—outside of its proximity to Olympic National Park—is clearly the city pier. An observation tower at pier's end provides 360-degree views of the city, harbor, and majestic Olympic mountains, while a sandy beach with picnic area is available for day use. Also located on the pier near the *Coho* ferry dock, the **Arthur D. Feiro Marine Laboratory** (360/417-6254, www.olypen.com/feirolab, noon–4 P.M. Sat.–Sun. year-round, 10 A.M.–8 P.M. daily in summer, $3 adults, $2 seniors, $1 for kids ages 3–17, and free for under age 2), operated by Peninsula College, has hands-on displays and exhibits of the area's sealife, with volunteers to answer questions. More than 80 species are here, including sea slugs, eels, octopuses, starfish, and sea urchins.

Waterfront Trail

Stop by the downtown visitors center for a walking-tour brochure that leads you through the historical sights of Port Angeles. The city's Waterfront Trail is a delightful six-mile paved path that follows the downtown shoreline and continues out to the Coast Guard base on **Ediz Hook**—a 3.5-mile-long natural sand spit protecting the Northwest's deepest harbor.

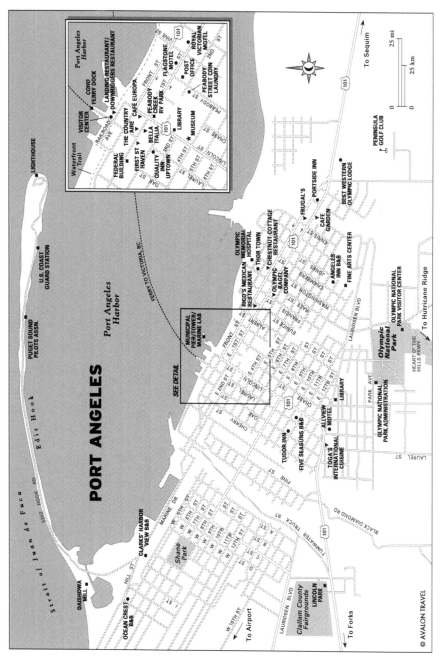

PORT ANGELES

Port Angeles Harbor

Strait of Juan de Fuca

Ediz Hook

LIGHTHOUSE

U.S. COAST GUARD STATION

PUGET SOUND PILOTS ASSN.

EDIZ HOOK RD

DAISHOWA MILL

OCEAN CREST B&B

CLARKS' HARBOR VIEW B&B

MARINE DR

HILL ST

Shane Park

W 9TH ST
W 7TH ST
W 6TH ST
W 8TH ST
W 9TH ST
W 10TH ST
W 11TH ST
W 12TH ST

I ST

C ST
C ST

W 18TH ST

To Airport

LAUHDSEN BLVD

Clallam County Fairgrounds

LINCOLN PARK

To Forks

BLACK DIAMOND RD

TUMWATER TRUCK RT

PINE ST

CHERRY ST

OAK ST

FERRY TO VICTORIA, BC

SEE DETAIL

MUNICIPAL PIER/TOWER/ MARINE LAB

FRONT ST

E 1ST ST
E 2ND ST
E 5TH ST
E 6TH ST
E 7TH ST
E 8TH ST
E 10TH ST
E 11TH ST
E 12TH ST

ALBERT ST

LINCOLN ST

LAUREL ST

CHASE ST

OLYMPIC MEMORIAL HOSPITAL

RICO'S MEXICAN RESTAURANT

OLYMPIC BAGEL COMPANY

THOR TOWN

CHESTNUT COTTAGE RESTAURANT

RACE ST
FRANCIS ST
EUNICE ST
JONES ST
WASHINGTON ST
CHAMBERS ST
ENNIS ST

FRUGAL'S

CAFE GARDEN

PORTSIDE INN

BEST WESTERN OLYMPIC LODGE

ANGELES INN B&B

FINE ARTS CENTER

LAUHDSEN BLVD

OLYMPIC NATIONAL PARK VISITOR CENTER

Olympic National Park

HEART O' THE HILLS PKWY

To Hurricane Ridge

PARK AVE

LIBRARY

OLYMPIC NATIONAL PARK ADMINISTRATION

LAUREL ST

ALLVIEW MOTEL

FIVE SEASONS B&B

TUDOR INN

TOGA'S INTERNATIONAL CUISINE

To Sequim

101

PENINSULA GOLF CLUB

25 mi

25 km

0

0

© AVALON TRAVEL

Port Angeles Harbor

DETAIL

Port Angeles Harbor

COHO FERRY DOCK

LANDING RESTAURANT/ DOWNRIGGERS RESTAURANT

FRONT ST
RAILROAD AVE

1ST ST
2ND ST

ENNIS ST

101

FLAGSTONE

POST OFFICE

ROYAL VICTORIAN MOTEL

PEABODY ST

PEABODY STREET COIN LAUNDRY

VISITOR CENTER

THE COUNTRY AIRE

CAFÉ EUROPA

PEABODY CREEK RV PARK

BELLA ITALIA

Waterfront Trail

FEDERAL BUILDING

FIRST ST HAVEN

QUALITY INN UPTOWN

OAK ST
LAUREL ST
LINCOLN ST
CHASE ST

3RD ST

LIBRARY

MUSEUM

7TH ST
8TH ST

Along the way you're treated to views across to Vancouver Island and back toward town with the snowcapped Olympics in the background. Watch as freighters are guided in, or take out your own boat for fishing or sightseeing. Picnicking and beachcombing are also popular activities. The U.S. Coast Guard Air Station occupies the far end of the spit and has the cutter *Active* docked at the city pier when it isn't out on rescue missions or drug searches. Located a short distance from the Coast Guard base, the Puget Sound Pilots Association assigns a pilot to each commercial ship passing this point to steer it on its way through Puget Sound. Another place offering fine vistas across to Vancouver Island is from the top of the Laurel Street stairs, two blocks uphill from the *Coho* ferry dock.

Port Angeles Fine Arts Center

The Port Angeles Fine Arts Center (1203 E. Lauridsen Blvd., 360/417-4590, www.pafac. org, 11 A.M.–5 P.M. Thurs.–Sun., free) is a bit out of the way, but well worth the side trip. Located on a hill, the building's enormous picture windows face north to Vancouver Island, offering panoramic vistas that pull your eyes away from the art on the walls. Walk outside to discover a small forest with gardens and a path leading to additional viewpoints. The Fine Arts Center features changing exhibits by prominent Northwest artists.

Olympic National Park Visitor Center

Located a mile out of town, the Olympic National Park Visitor Center (3002 Mt. Angeles Rd., 360/452-0330, www.nps.gov/olym, daily year-round) is an ideal first stop for visitors to Olympic National Park or the very popular Hurricane Ridge, 17 miles south of town. The center includes a large panoramic map, exhibits about the park, a Discovery Room for kids, and a 12-minute slide show that introduces visitors to the Olympics. Nature trails lead through the forest to park headquarters, a block away. Get backcountry information from the summer-only **Wilderness Information Center**

(directly behind the visitors center, 360/565-3100, www.nps.gov/olym/wic). Also here is the Beaumont log cabin, built in 1887 and moved here in 1962.

◖ Hurricane Ridge

One of the park's most scenic and most visited areas, Hurricane Ridge rises over 5,200 feet seemingly straight up from the Strait of Juan de Fuca, providing an awesome contrast from sea level and breathtaking 360-degree views. The paved road starts at Race Street in Port Angeles, becoming Mt. Angeles Road and then Hurricane Ridge Road as it snakes up mountainsides for 17 miles at an easy 7 percent grade; frequent turnouts allow for photo breaks. At the top, the **Hurricane Ridge Visitor Center** provides a must-stop location to peer across a meadow-and-mountain landscape that might have been imported straight from the Swiss Alps. This is one of the park's best areas for spotting wildlife; black-tailed deer often bound across the parking lot, marmots are found in nearby slopes, and black bears are occasionally visible from a distance. The ridge's name isn't without basis in fact: the first lodge at the summit lost its roof in a strong winter blast. The weather can change quickly up here; tune in to AM 530 in Port Angeles for weather and other park information.

Hurricane Ridge Visitor Center provides food service, a gift shop, winter ski rentals, and ski-tow service. It is usually open daily May–Sept., and on weekends only during October and mid-December through April. Park naturalists offer summertime walks and talks plus wintertime snowshoe treks. **Royal Victoria Tours**, 360/417-8006, offers three-hour (very hurried) bus tours up Hurricane Ridge daily at 1 P.M. from the ferry dock in Port Angeles; $21 adult, $12 kids age 5–16.

If the drop-offs and absence of guardrails on Hurricane Ridge Rd. made your palms sweat, you're in for a real treat on **Obstruction Point Road.** Starting from the Hurricane Ridge parking lot, this narrow gravel road (no RVs) follows the ridge for eight miles without a rail or fence, providing spectacular views for the

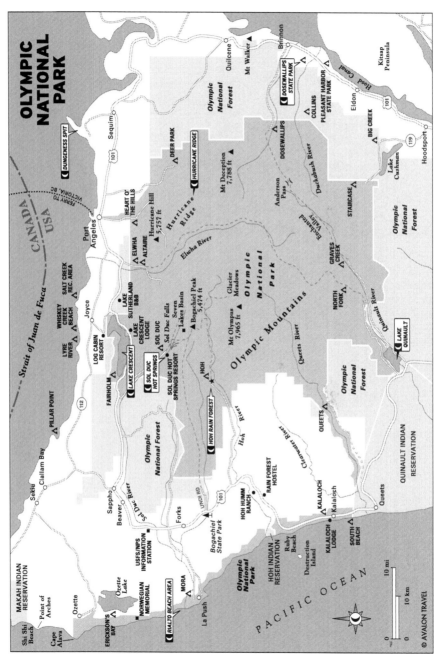

OLYMPIC NATIONAL PARK

Strait of Juan de Fuca

CANADA / USA

FERRY TO VICTORIA, BC

Shi Shi Beach
Point of Arches
Cape Alava
Ozette
MAKAH INDIAN RESERVATION
ERICKSON'S BAY
Ozette Lake
Sekiu
Clallam Bay
Pillar Point
Whiskey Creek Beach
Lyre River
Salt Creek Rec. Area
Joyce
Sappho
Beaver
Sol Duc River
Forks
USFS/NPS Information Station
NORWEGIAN MEMORIAL
RIALTO BEACH AREA
MORA
La Push
Bogachiel State Park
Olympic National Park
Rain Forest Hostel
Hoh Humm Ranch
HOH INDIAN RESERVATION
Ruby Beach
Destruction Island
KALALOCH LODGE
KALALOCH
Kalaloch
SOUTH BEACH
Queets
QUINAULT INDIAN RESERVATION
Olympic National Forest
LAKE QUINAULT
Quinault River
Queets River
QUEETS
Clearwater River
Hoh River
HOH RAIN FOREST
HOH
SOL DUC HOT SPRINGS RESORT
SOL DUC HOT SPRINGS
SOL DUC
Sol Duc Falls
LAKE CRESCENT LODGE
LAKE CRESCENT
FAIRHOLM
LOG CABIN RESORT
LAKE SUTHERLAND
B&B
Seven Lakes Basin
Bogachiel Peak 5,474 ft
Glacier Meadows
Mt Olympus 7,965 ft
Olympic Mountains
Olympic National Park
Elwha River
ELWHA
ALTAIRE
HEART O' THE HILLS
Hurricane Hill 5,757 ft
HURRICANE RIDGE
Hurricane Ridge
DEER PARK
Mt Deception 7,788 ft
Bailey Range
Port Angeles
DUNGENESS SPIT
Sequim
101
Quilcene
Mt Walker
BRinnon
DOSEWALLIPS STATE PARK
COLLINS
PLEASANT HARBOR STATE PARK
Eldon
Hood Canal
Kitsap Peninsula
Dosewallips River
Duckabush River
DOSEWALLIPS
Anderson Pass
Enchanted Valley
GRAVES CREEK
NORTH FORK
STAIRCASE
BIG CREEK
Lake Cushman
Hoodsport
119
Olympic National Forest
Olympic National Forest

PACIFIC OCEAN

10 mi
10 km
0

© AVALON TRAVEL

strong-hearted. The road, constructed in the 1930s by the Civilian Conservation Corps, went as far as it could until a steep talus slope prohibited any further road-making.

ENTERTAINMENT AND EVENTS
Nightlife
Six miles west of town, **Annie M's Junction** (242701 W. Hwy. 101, 360/452-9880) offers occasional live music.

Check out the big screen at **Lincoln Theater** (132 E. 1st St., 360/457-7997) for the latest flicks.

The Arts
The **Port Angeles Symphony Orchestra** (360/457-5579, www.olypen.com/pasymphony) performs six concerts during the winter months. The **Port Angeles Light Opera Association** (360/457-5630, www.paloa.org) produces a musical each July. Live theater performances are given by **Port Angeles Community Players** (360/452-665, www.pacommunityplayers.com) year-round at the playhouse on Lauridsen Boulevard and Liberty Street.

Festivals and Events
The **4th of July** brings music at the pier, kids' events, and a big fireworks show off the beach. The **Clallam County Fair** comes to Port Angeles the third weekend of August, with a carnival, rodeo, horse shows, farming exhibits, and a crowd-pleasing smash-'em-up demolition derby.

Each Memorial Day weekend, the **Juan de Fuca Festival** (360/457-5411, www.juandefucafestival.com) features a wide range of music, dance, comedy, kids' activities, arts and crafts, food, and more. For something a bit less formal, free **Concerts on the Pier** (360/452-2363) take place every Thursday evening mid-June to mid-September.

Another popular event is the **Forest Storytelling Festival** (360/417-5031), which attracts tale-tellers from the U.S. and Canada in late September or early October. End the

year in style with a visit to the **Christmas Crafts Fair** on the first weekend of December, where local artisans display their works.

SHOPPING
Arts and Crafts
Port Angeles's downtown shopping district is centered on 1st Street, where you'll find shops, restaurants, galleries, and movie theaters. Several galleries carry artwork by local artists with Northwestern themes, including **Waterfront Gallery** (Landing Mall, 360/452-8165, 10 A.M.–5:30 P.M. daily) and **Olympic Stained Glass** (112 N. Laurel, 360/457-1090, 10 A.M.–5:30 P.M. Mon.–Sat., closed Sun.). For something completely different, head to **Pacific Rim Hobby** (124-A W. 1st St., 360/457-0794 or 800/994-6229, 10 A.M.–6 P.M. Mon.–Sat., noon–5 P.M. Sun.) for a voyage to model railroad heaven. The big HO-scale railroad village makes for fun gawking; look for such details as the giant insect attacking villagers.

Bookstores
Port Angeles has three good bookstores: **Odyssey Bookshop** (114 W. Front St., 360/457-1045, 9 A.M.–7 P.M. Mon.–Sat., 10 A.M.–5 P.M. Sun.), **Port Book and News** (104 E. 1st, 360/452-6367, 8 A.M.–8 P.M. Mon.–Sat., 8 A.M.–5 P.M. Sun.) and **Olympic Stationers** (122 E. Front St., 360/457-6111, 8:30 A.M.5:30 P.M. Mon.–Fri., 10 A.M.–3 P.M. Sat., closed Sun.).

Outdoor Gear
Port Angeles is an ideal spot to gear up before venturing afield within the national park and the rest of the Olympic National Forest. Find a good selection of outdoor gear for sale at **Browns Outdoor** (112 W Front St., 360/457-4150, www.brownsoutdoor.com), including often forgotten essentials such as stove fuel, dehydrated goodies, and the like.

SPORTS AND RECREATION
Racing
From early April to mid-October, **Port Angeles Speedway**, 360/452-4666, six miles

east of Port Angeles on Hwy. 101, has stock- and hobby-car races on Saturday nights.

Winter Sports
Between late December and late March, Hurricane Ridge is a popular winter destination for cross-country and downhill skiers, snowboarders, and tubers. A small **ski area** (360/452-0330) has two rope tows and a Poma lift. It's open on weekends and during the Christmas–New Year's holiday. Ski rentals, including cross-country and Telemark packages, are also available, along with ski lessons. Backcountry skiers will discover a wealth of open country at Hurricane Ridge—check avalanche conditions before heading out.

Park Service naturalists (360/452-0330) offer guided snowshoe walks on weekends and other times in the winter. Snowshoes are provided ($2 donation suggested). The visitors center—where you can warm up—and cafeteria are open winter weekends. The road to the top is open 9 A.M.–dusk Sat.–Mon. and is closed overnight or during storms. Entrance fees are charged on weekends. Call ahead (360/452-0329) for current road and weather conditions, and always come prepared for the worst. No overnight parking at the summit.

Swimming
Swim at the **William Shore Memorial Pool** (225 E. 5th St., 360/457-4595). For lake swimming, head a dozen miles west of town to **Lake Sutherland,** where the water gets quite warm by late summer.

Bike and Kayak Rentals
Rent mountain and road bikes along with kayaks from **Sound Bikes and Kayaks** (120 E. Front St., 360/457-1240, www.sound-bikeskayaks.com, 10 A.M.–6 P.M. Mon.–Sat., closed Sun.). Bikes are $9 for the first hour, $5 per additional hour, or $30 for the day. **Beckett's Bike Shop** (117 W. 1st. St., 360/452-0842, www.beckettsbikeshop.com, 10 A.M.–5 P.M. Mon.–Sat., closed Sun.) has a great selection of bikes and parts and organizes weekly group rides.

Hiking
A number of trails begin at Hurricane Ridge, including 1.5-mile **Hurricane Hill Trail,** a paved walk to the top of 5,757-foot Hurricane Hill that passes picnic areas, marmot colonies, and spectacular vistas. A longer hike, the **Klahanee Ridge Trail,** follows the ridge's summit for four miles after leaving the paved trail near the marmot colonies. It continues downhill to Heart O' the Hills Campground, or you can return back to Hurricane Ridge.

In addition to these, visitors to Hurricane Ridge will find three other short paved trails through the flower-filled meadows with views of the Olympics. Longer paths lead downhill to the Elwha Valley and along the Little River. From Obstruction Peak, additional trails provide access into the heart of the Olympics.

Camping
No camping or overnight lodging is available at Hurricane Ridge, but several options are nearby. **Heart O' the Hills Campground** (five miles south of Port Angeles on Hurricane Ridge Rd., $12) has year-round camping, with campfire programs are offered July through Labor Day. Located at an elevation of 5,400 feet, **Deer Park Campground** ($8, mid-June to late September) sits at the end of a narrow 18-mile gravel road on the eastern edge of the park. No RVs are permitted, and it is not accessible from the Hurricane Ridge area.

Near the airport, **Lincoln Park's** (W. Lauridsen Blvd. and Bean Rd.) authentic pioneer cabins and a longhouse accompany tennis courts, baseball diamond, campsites ($8 tent and RV, no hookups), nature trails, picnic area, and children's fishing pond at this 144-acre park. Campers can use the showers at the local swimming pool (225 E. 5th St.) or the boat harbor.

RV owners hoping to catch a ferry to Victoria may find **Peabody Creek RV Park** (127 S. Lincoln, 360/457-7092 or 800/392-2361, $27 with full hookups) convenient. This very basic park isn't much more than a parking lot with utilities, but it is right next to the docks.

For a few more amenities, try **Conestoga**

Quarters RV Park (40 Sieberts Creek Rd., 360/452-4637 or 800/808-4637, $25 with full hookups), which—in spite of cramped spaces—offers an off-leash area for dogs, showers, laundry facilities, free Wi-Fi, and a clubhouse. Also in town, **Crescent Beach RV** (2860 Crescent Beach Rd., 360/928-3344 or 866/690-3344, $40 with full hookups) is another pet-friendly private campground that offers access to a long, sandy beach, along with coin-op showers and laundry, plus a convenience store.

ACCOMMODATIONS

Because of the popularity of Port Angeles in the summer months, it's a good idea to make reservations ahead of your visit. Stop by the visitors center to check the board for availability at local motels, B&Bs, and RV parks, or to use its phone to make reservations. The chamber of commerce website (www.cityofpa.com) has links to most local lodging places. Many of these offer free transport from the airport or ferry terminal upon request.

Under $100

The best deal in Port Angeles can be found at **Thor Town** (316 N. Race St., 360/452-0931, www.thortown.com, $14 dorm bed, $30 d private room), a free-spirited hostel set in a red barn-style farmhouse. Guests can make use of laundry facilities and the full kitchen, with the choice of buying food here or hopping on one of the hostel's rental bikes and picking up grub at the grocery store. This hostel has no lockout hours during the day.

Another value-minded option is **All-View Motel** (214 E. Lauridsen Blvd., 360/457-7779, www.allviewmotel.com, $49–99 d), a frayed-at-the-edges mom-and-pop motel that makes a decent overnighter. Kitchenettes are available in some units.

Flagstone Motel (415 E. 1st St., 360/457-9494 or 888/304-3465, www.flagstonemotel.net, $49 s or $69 d) is a centrally located motel with an indoor pool and sauna; continental breakfast is included.

Perched on a hilltop, rooms at the **Quality Inn Uptown** (101 E. 2nd St., 360/457-9434 or 800/858-3812, $85–96 s or d) all have lots of light streaming through the floor-to-ceiling windows, with peekaboo views of the harbor and mountains. Rooms are pretty worn, but the hot breakfast, friendly staff, and reasonable rates balance this out a bit. Plus, the property is dog friendly.

The three-story **Portside Inn** (1510 E. Front St., 360/452-4015 or 877/438-8588, www.portsideinn.com, $49–89 d) has fairly standard motel rooms, plus an outdoor pool and hot tub.

$100-150

A small family hotel on a hill right in downtown, **Port Angeles Inn** (111 E. 2nd St., 360/452-9285 or 800/421-0706, www.portangelesinn.com, $59–175 s or d) has comfortable rooms, many with panoramic views over the harbor.

Also with impressive views of the mountains and water is **Best Western Olympic Lodge** (140 Del Guzzi Dr., 360/452-2993 or 800/600-2993, www.portangeleshotelmotel.com, $116–197 s or d), with spacious rooms and continental breakfast. The hotel has an outdoor pool, hot tub, exercise room, and free airport and ferry shuttles.

Ocean Crest B&B (402 S. M St., 360/452-4832 or 877/413-2169, www.oceancrestbnb.com, $75–95 s or d), a mile west of Port Angeles looking down on the waterfront, has three tasteful bedrooms with private baths and free transportation to and from the ferry. Kids are accepted.

Tudor Inn B&B (1108 S. Oak, 360/452-3138, www.tudorinn.com, $125–160 s or d, discount for active-duty U.S. armed forces) is a 1910 half-timbered English Tudor home with five pretty guest rooms featuring crown molding; one has a canopied bed. Mountain and water views come at no additional charge. Most rooms have private baths.

The Five SeaSuns B&B (1006 S. Lincoln, 360/452-8248, www.seasuns.com, $90–165 s or d) is a grand 1926 Dutch Colonial home on spacious grounds. Inside are five guest rooms, shared or private baths, and period furnishings.

$150-200
Inn at Rooster Hill B&B (112 Reservoir Rd., 360/452-4933, www.innatroosterhill.com, $149–189 s or d) is a five-bedroom country house in the foothills of mountains outside of town.

$200-250
Located halfway between Port Angeles and Sequim, **(Domaine Madeleine** (146 Wildflower Ln., 360/457-4174, www.domaine-madeleine.com, $195–310 s or d) is an elegant waterfront estate overlooking the Strait of Juan de Fuca. The four guest rooms and a separate cottage (perfect for honeymooners) are luxuriously appointed, and a multicourse epicurean breakfast starts your day. The innkeepers speak French in addition to English.

FOOD
Because of its location as a jumping-off point for Olympic National Park and Vancouver Island, Port Angeles is packed with high-quality eateries of all persuasions.

Cafés and Diners
The acclaimed **First Street Haven** (1st and Laurel, 360/457-0352, 7 A.M.–4 P.M. daily, 8 A.M.–2 P.M. Sun.) serves hearty breakfasts, along with reasonable sandwiches, quiche, pastas, and salads for lunch. The location is tiny, but the food is hard to beat and on Sundays you can gorge on breakfast all day long. The same owners run the equally popular **Chestnut Cottage Restaurant** (929 E Front St., 360/452-8344, 7 A.M.–3 P.M. daily) featuring creative egg dishes for breakfast, plus salads, pastas, fajitas, and burgers for lunch. The setting is cozy and friendly.

Another fine breakfast and lunch spot is **(Cafe Garden** (1506 E. 1st St., 360/457-4611, 6:30 A.M.–2:30 P.M. daily) where the menu covers the spectrum from Belgium waffles for breakfast to Asian stir-fries and deli sandwiches for lunch.

Good breakfasts, along with the best local fish and chips, can be found at **Landing Restaurant** (115 E. Railroad Ave., 360/457-6768, 7 A.M.–9 P.M. daily).

Get the best burgers and fries anywhere around at **Frugals** (1520 E. Front St., 360/452-4320, 10:30 A.M.–10 P.M. Sun.–Thurs., 10:30 A.M.–11 P.M. Fri.–Sat.). There's no seating—just drive up or walk up to order.

Steak and Seafood
A popular steak and seafood restaurant overlooking the water is **Downriggers Restaurant** (115 E. Railroad, 360/452-2700, 11:30 A.M.–9 P.M. Sun.–Thurs., 11:30 A.M.–9:30 P.M. Fri.–Sat.). **The Bushwacker Restaurant** (1527 E. 1st, 360/457-4113, 4:30–9 P.M. daily) specializes in fresh seafood and prime rib and also has a good salad bar. Open for dinner only.

International
For tasty, reasonably priced, and authentic south-of-the-border meals, visit **Rico's Mexican Restaurant** (636 E. Front St., 360/452-3928, 11 A.M.–9:30 P.M. daily), with an extensive menu and daily specials. Housed in a cozy Victorian-era home, **(Toga's International Cuisine** (122 W. Lauridsen Blvd., 360/452-1952) specializes in upscale German and Hungarian dinners, but also includes Northwest seafood. This place is very nice, but expensive.

Four miles east of Port Angeles, **C'est Si Bon** (23 Cedar Park Dr., 360/452-8888, 5–9 P.M. Tues.–Sun., closed Mon., entrées $20–25) prepares delicious local seafood with a French accent. The Olympics and rose garden views add to the luxurious ambiance.

Located downstairs from an organic grocery, **Bella Italia** (117B E. 1st St., 360/457-5442, 4–10 P.M. Mon.–Sat., 4–8:45 P.M. Sun.) blends traditional Italian cooking with a natural foods sensibility. The result is easily Port Angeles' finest Italian restaurant, with great desserts, too.

Bakeries
Pick up the freshest bagel on the peninsula with loads of cream cheese or filled up sandwich style at **Olympic Bagel Company** (802

E 1st St., 360/452-9100, www.olympicbagel.
com, 6 A.M.–4 P.M. Mon.–Sat., 7 A.M.–3 P.M.
Sun., winter hours may vary), which serves
lots of breakfast and lunch items, plus Tully's
coffee.

Markets
Get the freshest local fare at **Port Angeles
Farmers Market** (360/683-4642, 9 A.M.–
3:30 P.M. Sat.) held year-round near the corner of 8th and Chase Streets. **Sunny Farms
Country Store** (360/683-8003) has a large
produce stand located halfway between Port
Angeles and Sequim. Also sold here: everything
from hanging plants to homemade pizzas.

    The Country Aire (117 E. 1st St., 360/452-
7175, 9 A.M.–7 P.M. Mon.–Sat., 11 A.M.–4 P.M.
Sun.) has a big selection of natural and organic
foods. For the freshest local seafood—along
with canned and smoked specialties—stop by
Hegg & Hegg (801 Marine Dr., 360/457-3344,
9 A.M.–6 P.M. Mon.–Sat., 10 A.M.–5 P.M. Sun.).
They also have a small gift shop in the Landing
Mall, where the ferry docks (360/457-3733).

INFORMATION AND SERVICES
For maps, brochures, and more local information, contact the **Port Angeles Chamber of
Commerce Visitor Center** (121 E. Railroad
Ave., 360/452-2363, www.cityofpa.com,
8 A.M.–9 P.M. daily Memorial Day–mid-Sept.,
10 A.M.–4 P.M. daily the rest of the year).

    Just a few steps away is the **Port Angeles-
Victoria Tourist Bureau** (360/452-1223,
7 A.M.–5 P.M. daily). Here the focus is on
travel, motel, and B&B reservations for southwest British Columbia—particularly nearby
Vancouver Island—but they can also make
motel reservations for Port Angeles. Tons
of British Columbia maps and brochures
are free for the taking. Both the chamber of
commerce and the tourist bureau are excep-
tionally helpful. Another source of information is the **North Olympic Peninsula Visitor
and Convention Bureau** (338 W. 1st. St.,
360/452-8552, www.olympus.net).

    The **Olympic National Park Visitor
Center** (3002 Mt. Angeles Rd., 360/452-0330)
can give you sightseeing, hiking, camping, and
other park information.

    Campers and backpackers will appreci-
ate **Peabody Street Coin Laundry** (212 S.
Peabody, 24 hours daily) after getting back to
nature in Olympic National Park. **The Spa**
(511 E. 1st St., 360/452-3257 or 800/869-7177)
has been around since 1928, with Finnish-style
steam rooms, massage, herbal body wraps, and
a juice bar and tearoom. (The hostel is also
here.)

GETTING THERE AND AROUND
By Ferry
Port Angeles is a major transit point for travelers heading to or from Victoria, B.C., just 18
miles away across the Strait of Juan de Fuca.
The MV *Coho* (360/457-4491, www.cohoferry.
com, $47.50 one-way for car and driver, $12.50
for passengers, $6.25 for kids 5–11, free under
age 5, and $17.75 for bicycle and rider) sails
on a 90-minute run between Port Angeles and
Victoria four times daily in summer (mid-May
through October), and twice daily the rest of
the year. For specific departure times, contact the Black Ball ferry terminal at the foot
of Laurel Street in Port Angeles. Vehicle space
is at a premium on summer weekends and no
reservations are accepted; get there very early
to be assured of passage. Another option is to
park your car in one of the lots near the ferry
terminal ($10/day) and take the *Victoria Express*
over. The *Coho* is out of service for mainte-
nance from early January to early March.

    The *Victoria Express* (360/452-8088 or
800/633-1589, www.victoriaexpress.com,
$12.50 one-way, $5 bicycles and kayaks), a passenger-only ferry, makes the same run in an
hour, two or three times a day from late May to
early October. The ferry departs the Landing
Mall terminal in Port Angeles. Advance reservations are advised July–Labor Day.

By Air
Horizon Airlines (800/547-9308) provides
daily commuter service to Victoria, B.C., and

to Sea-Tac Airport from Fairchild International Airport on the city's west side. **Harbor Air** (800/359-3220) also flies to Sea-Tac.

Rite Bros. Aviation (360/452-6226) offers flightseeing and charter flights over the Olympics from Port Angeles.

By Bus

Public bus service now extends throughout the Olympic Peninsula, making it possible to reach all the towns for a minimal fare on any of the four different public transit systems. **Clallam Transit** (360/452-4511 or 800/858-3747, www.clallamtransit.com) provides Monday–Saturday service around the Olympic Peninsula to Forks, Neah Bay, La Push, and Olympic National Park's Sol Duc Hot Springs and Lake Crescent. The buses have bike racks. They also connect with **Jefferson Transit** (360/385-4777 or 800/773-7788, www.jeffersontransit.com) in Sequim for Port Townsend and other Jefferson County points, and with **Grays Harbor Transit** in Queets for points to the south.

Olympic Bus Lines (360/417-0700 or 800/457-4492, www.olympicbuslines.com) offers van service connecting Port Angeles with Seattle and Sea-Tac Airport.

Port Angeles to Sol Duc

ELWHA RIVER VALLEY

Take Olympic Hot Springs Road south from Highway 101 just west of Port Angeles into the Elwha River watershed, best known for a bulwark project currently underway to demolish two dams and restore the river to its former pristine state. This river valley offers some of the closest remote hiking, camping, and rafting to Port Angeles.

Sports and Recreation
RIVER RAFTING

With Class II white-water conditions, The Elwha River is a popular destination for riverrunners of all experience levels. Check with the Park Service for current flow conditions and precautions if you decide to run it yourself. **Olympic Raft and Guide Service** (360/452-1443, www.northolympic.com/olympicraft) leads scenic two-hour trips down the Elwha River ($49 adults, $39 kids), plus sea kayaking in Lake Crescent, Lake Aldwell, and Freshwater Bay.

HIKING

Nearly everyone in Washington knows of Sol Duc Hot Springs, but less well known are **Olympic Hot Springs,** located at the end of Boulder Creek Rd., off Elwha River Road. The springs were once the site of a large resort, but today they are essentially undeveloped. A 2.5-mile trail leads to shallow rock-lined pools, where the water varies from lukewarm to 138°F. The Park Service discourages bathing and prohibits nudity (but that doesn't stop many folks from bathing au naturel).

Take the Elwha River Trail for two miles to **Humes Ranch,** built in 1889 by Grant Humes, who made his living leading wilderness expeditions and by hunting and trapping game. Today his cabin is on the National Register of Historic Places.

When a day hike is not enough, a number of hiking trails head into the backcountry from the Elwha area, and a variety of short and long hikes are available, including an across-the-park route that follows the Elwha Trail to Low Divide and then drops down to Quinault Lake on the North Quinault Trail, a distance of 44 miles.

For a north–south 44-mile trek, start at Lake Mills near Elwha on the **Elwha River Trail.** The trail runs 27.5 miles until it links up at Low Divide with the **North Fork Trail,** which follows the North Fork Quinault River until you reach the North Fork Ranger Station near Lake Quinault. You'll be hiking the route of James Halbold Christie, leader of the *Seattle*

Press expedition across the then-unexplored Olympic Peninsula. It took Christie and his party six months and one black bear to complete the route in 1890; it should take you only four days and a packful of gorp.

CAMPING
Pitch your tent at the Elwha and Altaire campgrounds ($12) along the road north of Lake Mills (created by Glines Canyon Dam).

Accommodations
Situated in a country home overlooking the Elwha River valley, **Elwha Ranch B&B** (360/457-6540, www.elwharanch.com, $140–150 d) has two guest rooms with private baths, a deck, and full breakfasts. The property features a private log cabin ($165) for those seeking a bit more seclusion.

◖ LAKE CRESCENT
According to Native American legend, Mount Storm King once became so fed up with the fighting between the Clallams and Quileutes that he broke a rock off his head and threw it down at the warring tribes. The scientific view of the Lake Crescent's origin isn't much different; it's attributed to ancient landslides that divided a glacial lake into two large sections (Lake Crescent and Lake Sutherland), sending water from Lake Crescent out the Lyre River. However you look at it, Lake Crescent is an azure jewel set amid the emerald forests.

Sights and Recreation
Today, freshwater Lake Crescent, 624 feet deep and 8.5 miles long, is famous for its Beardslee trout, a subspecies that is large (some are in the 12–14 pound range) and a hard fighter when hooked. Swimming, boating, camping, picnicking, and, of course, fishing are popular lake activities. The lake has an impressive mountain-rimmed setting. The Park Service's **Storm King Ranger Station** (360/928-3380) is staffed during the summer months.

The nonprofit **Olympic Park Institute**

Lake Crescent on Olympic Peninsula, near Port Angeles

© WASHINGTON STATE TOURISM/JIM POTH

(360/928-3720 or 800/775-3720, www.yni. org/opi) offers excellent hands-on field seminars covering such diverse topics as Makah basketry, ecology of the forest canopy, and wolf biology. Seminars last 2–5 days and some may be taken for college credit. They also have an Elderhostel. Headquarters for the institute is the historic Rosemary Inn, near Lake Crescent Lodge. Students stay in nearby cabins, and meals are served family style at the inn.

HIKING
From the ranger station, follow the **Marymere Falls Trail** 0.75 mile for a spectacular view of this 90-foot falls. Not a lot of water, but it's quite impressive nevertheless. Return via the Crescent Lake Lodge Trail for a two-mile loop hike.

The **Mt. Storm King Trail** splits off from the Marymere Trail and climbs more than 3,000 feet in a bit over a mile, with fine views across the lake. The path ends before the summit, and the Park Service recommends against continuing to the top due to hazardous conditions.

A four-mile hike starting at Lyre River Road or North Shore Road at opposite ends of Lake Crescent, the **Spruce Railroad Trail** follows the tracks of the 1918 Spruce Railroad, built to supply spruce for World War I aircraft. The war was over before the railroad was completed, however, and the spruce was no longer needed. Two tunnels (closed) and depressions from the railroad ties remain. Besides a taste of local history, the almost-level hike provides a view of Lake Crescent.

CAMPING
Fairholm Campground ($12; open year-round), on the west end of Lake Crescent, has summertime naturalist programs on some evenings. The Forest Service's **Klahowya Campground** (nine miles west of Lake Crescent on Hwy. 101, $12) opens sites May to mid-October.

Park RVs along Lake Sutherland at **Shadow Mt. RV Park** (360/928-3043).

Fairholm General Store (360/928-3020) on the west end of Lake Crescent, is open

April–September, and has tent sites and RV hookups, plus motorboats, rowboats, and canoes for rent. It also serves meals in the café; eat alfresco on a deck overlooking the lake.

Accommodations
The lake has two concession-operated lodges around its perimeter. Built in 1916, ◖ **Lake Crescent Lodge** (360/928-3211, www. olypen.com/lakecrescentlodge, $99–158 d lodge, $180–231 cottages, Apr.–Oct. only) is a cozy place with a comfortable feeling from decades of guests, including President Franklin D. Roosevelt, who stayed here in 1937. Sit on the porch for incredible views of the mountains and Lake Crescent, or lounge in front of the big fireplace on a cool evening. The lodge has all sorts of accommodations, including lodge rooms (bath down the hall), cottages (some with fireplaces), and modern motel units. The lodge has a restaurant and gift shop, and rents rowboats.

Rent out motel rooms, rustic cabins, or waterfront A-frame chalets at **Log Cabin Resort** (three miles from Hwy. 101 on E. Beach Rd., 360/928-3325, www.logcabinresort.net, $89–145 d, Apr.–Oct. only) at the northeast end of the lake. There are also camping cabins ($55) available for those with simple tastes. Many of the buildings have stood here since the 1920s. In addition to accommodations, the resort also has meals, a gift shop, grocery store, RV and tent sites, and rowboat, paddleboat, canoe, and kayak rentals.

East of Lake Crescent is the smaller Lake Sutherland, a popular place to swim. **Lake Sutherland Lodge B&B** (360/928-2111 or 888/231-1444, $65–90 s or d) is a modern log home with a covered deck facing the lake. The four guest rooms have private or shared baths, and a full breakfast is served.

SOL DUC
The wild and free Sol Duc River Valley offers hikers a chance to go deep into the mystical Olympic forests, experience soothing hot springs, and take a gander at one of the prettiest waterfalls on the peninsula.

Recreation
◀ SOL DUC HOT SPRINGS
About 30 miles west of Port Angeles and 12 miles south of Highway 101, is Sol Duc (SOLE duck) hot springs (9 A.M.–9 P.M. daily mid-May through Aug., till 8 P.M. in Sept., 9 A.M.–8 P.M. Sat.–Sun. Apr.–mid-May, and Oct., $10 adults, $6.50 two hours or less before closing, $7.50 seniors). Bask in the 99–105°F mineral water piped into three large outdoor pools. A fourth freshwater pool is also on the site. Massage is also available.

FISHING
Sol Duc is legendary for its steelhead fishing in winter, plus year-round chinook and king salmon fisheries. Avoid the hassle of schlepping your own gear and schedule a trip with **Piscatorial Pursuits** (800/347-4232, www.piscatorialpursuits.com, $300 per person per day), which provides guidance based on years of reading the river, a boat, and all the tackle necessary to land one for the record books. The guide even cleans the fish for you.

HIKING
Several trails head up the Sol Duc Valley. A favorite is the one-mile **Sol Duc River Trail,** which passes through enormous western hemlocks and Douglas firs to Sol Duc Falls, one of the state's best-known waterfalls. A footbridge crosses the deep gorge cut by the river. From here, you can climb another three miles (one-way) to **Deer Lake,** bordered by trees. For variety, return to the campground from Sol Duc Falls on the **Lovers Lane Trail,** a three-mile path along the south side of the river.

A fine loop trip for backpackers (wilderness permit required) is to head up the Sol Duc River Trail to Seven Lakes Basin, then uphill to the summit of Bogachiel Peak and back out for a round-trip of 22 miles.

Practicalities
The springs were long known to the native peoples who first lived here, and white settlers were attracted to the area as a place of healing.

By 1912, the area had an elegant hotel, theater, bowling alley, a 100-bed sanitorium, plus immaculately landscaped grounds with a golf course, tennis courts, and croquet grounds. A fire, begun by a defective flue, brought this to a crashing halt four years later. As the hotel burned to the ground, a short circuit caused the player organ to begin playing Beethoven's "Funeral March."

Today's ◀ **Sol Duc Hot Springs Resort** (360/327-3583, www.northolympic.com/sol-duc, $141–172 d, mid-May–Sept. only) isn't quite so lavish, but it does have a restaurant, grocery store, and gift shop, plus cabins (some with kitchenettes). A two-night minimum applies on holidays.

Outdoor lovers may prefer to pitch a tent at the Park Service's **Sol Duc Campground** ($12), open all year, but sometimes closed in the winter months due to flooding. Between July and Labor Day, park naturalists offer evening programs in the amphitheater some evenings.

Partway between Sol Duc and Forks, **Bear Creek Motel** (15 miles northeast of Forks in the town of Beaver, 360/327-3660, www.hungrybearcafemotel.com, $50–85 d, $20 RV, $7 tent) makes a good stop for Olympic loop adventurers who just can't bear to drive past another mile marker. The **Hungry Bear Café** (5 A.M.–8 P.M. daily) here also makes a handy mealtime pitstop.

STRAIT OF JUAN DE FUCA
Highway 112 offers one of the most dramatic shoreline drives in Washington; the narrow road winds along cliff faces and past extraordinary views. The area is windswept and remote—the only radio stations to be found are from Canada—and the ocean is up close and personal much of the drive. At the end of the road, 72 miles from Port Angeles, Neah Bay sits on the 44-square-mile **Makah Indian Reservation** in virtual isolation, at the northwesternmost point of the contiguous United States. Anyone who has spent time in a remote Alaskan village will feel right at home in Neah Bay.

Sights
SALT CREEK COUNTY PARK
The scenic and diverse grounds at Salt Creek County Park (three miles east of Joyce off Hwy. 112, 360/928-3441) is an open secret among Washingtonians. This is, hands down, the nicest municipal park on the peninsula. Situated three miles east of the village of Joyce, this was the site of Fort Hayden during World War II, and the concrete gun emplacements are still explorable, though the 45-foot-long guns are long gone. The fort sits on a bluffside, with grassy lawns and picnic areas adjoining campsites. A path down to the rocky beach offers lots of tidepools during low tide. Farther up the bluff are several miles worth of trails.

OTHER PARKS
The beaches beyond Slip Point Lighthouse, on the east end of Clallam Bay, are great for beachcombing and exploring the tidepools, and the area east of here is famous for its marine fossils. County parks in the Clallam Bay area are **Clallam Bay Spit,** a 33-acre waterfront park for day use only, and **Pillar Point County Park** (360/963-2301), just east of Clallam Bay. Pillar Point is a four-acre park with a boat launch.

MAKAH MUSEUM
In 1970, tidal erosion unearthed old Ozette homes that had been destroyed by a mud slide some 500 years earlier. The slide entombed and preserved the material, and 11 years of excavations by archaeologists from Washington State University unearthed one of the richest finds in North America. Find thousands of these artifacts at the Makah Museum (Hwy. 112 & Bay View Ave., 360/645-2711, www.makah.com, 10 A.M.–5 P.M. daily Memorial Day–September 15; closed the rest of the year, $5 adults, $4 seniors and students) at Neah Bay. This is the finest collection of Northwest Coast Native American artifacts from pre-contact times, with an extraordinary range of material, including beautifully carved seal clubs, spears, bentwood boxes, combs, paddles, bows and arrows, clothing, woven baskets, whale bones, and much more. Not on display—it is too fragile—but visible in photos is an intricate plaid blanket woven from woodpecker feathers, dog hair, cattail fluff, and cedar bark. A re-created 15th-century longhouse is the museum's centerpiece, showing how the people lived in the abundance of the land. Outside, a modern longhouse is sometimes used for basketry and carving demonstrations.

An hour-long video about Neah Bay and the archaeological dig is shown at 11 A.M. and 2 P.M. daily. The small gift shop sells local baskets and beadwork. You can also obtain local information here.

Events
Makah Days is the town's big annual festival, celebrating the day the reservation first raised the American flag in 1913. Held on the weekend closest to August 26, the three-day festival is highlighted by dances, a parade, fireworks show, salmon bake, canoe races, and bone games (Native American gambling). Also popular is the **Chito Beach Bluegrass Jamboree** in mid-June.

Sports and Recreation
CAPE FLATTERY
The **Cape Loop Road** provides an interesting drive or mountain bike ride to the tip of Cape Flattery. The narrow dirt road is not for RVs. Pick up a route map at the museum, or head west from town to the Makah Tribal Center, and then turn right to the cape (left will take you to Hobuck Beach and a fish hatchery). About eight miles from town, you'll come to one of the few unlogged areas remaining on the cape, and the new **Cape Flattery Trail.** This fine boardwalk path leads downhill 0.75 mile to the rocky shoreline, with views of Tatoosh Island and **Cape Flattery Lighthouse,** built in 1858. Most folks return to Neah Bay the same way they came out, but mountain bikers and four-wheelers will enjoy the very rough road that leads back eastward around the cape to Neah Bay, passing a small waterfall with sculpted pools large enough to sit in on a warm summer day, and several miles later a dump

that has to be one of the worst in the state of Washington (but a good place to look for ravens and eagles). The total length of this loop is approximately 16 miles.

POINT OF ARCHES AND SHI SHI BEACH

Near the north park boundary, Point of Arches is a testimony to the relentless power of the Pacific where, with a force of two tons per square inch, the ocean carved giant arches out of ancient rock. The Arches, legendary children of Destruction Island and Tatoosh Island, were pushed from Mother Tatoosh's canoe when she deserted her husband because, she said, "You'd probably grow up just like your father!" The bluffs above neighboring Shi Shi (shy-shy) Beach provide a vantage point for watching the spring and fall gray whale migrations; the best viewing season is March–May. This stretch of coastline features some of the finest beaches and tidepools anywhere on the Washington coast; you might even find remains of a shipwreck still visible.

OZETTE LAKE AREA

Located in the northwest corner of the coastal strip, eight-mile-long Lake Ozette is the third-largest natural lake in Washington. A 21-mile paved road heads southwest from Sekiu, ending at the **Ozette Ranger Station** on the north end of the lake (360/963-2725, open daily in summer, no set hours in winter). This area has one of the most popular overnight hikes along the Olympic coast, and summer weekends attract outdoor enthusiasts. Parking costs $2 per day.

Two trails head to the coast from the ranger station. One leads southwest to **Sand Point,** three miles away; the other goes three miles northwest to **Cape Alva**—the westernmost point in the Lower 48. By hiking the beach connecting the two, you can create a triangular loop trip of 9.3 miles. You can also continue south on the beach for 2.3 miles to the **Norwegian Memorial,** a tribute to the victims of a 1903 shipwreck. There is much to explore in the Cape Alva area: fascinating tidepools, cannonball shaped rocks, an anchor from one

of the ships that ran aground here, and even an occasional Japanese glass ball. This is probably the best place to see wildlife in Olympic National Park, with bald eagles in the air, deer along the beach, sea lions and seals in the water, and migrating gray whales in fall and spring. This area contains the largest population of sea otters in the Lower 48; look for them in the kelp beds off Sand Point. The Wedding Rocks area between Cape Alva and Sand Point is well known for its petroglyphs, carved by the original inhabitants of this land at an unknown time. Pick up a handout describing the petroglyphs from the ranger station.

Practicalities
ALONG HIGHWAY 112

Right on the river and only a few steps from the Strait of Juan de Fuca, **Lyre River Recreation Area** offers free primitive campsites year-round. The best camping choice on the entire Strait, though, is at ◖ **Salt Creek County Park** (three miles east of Joyce off Hwy. 112, 360/928-3441, $24 full hookups, $18 tent), a gorgeous park that accommodates tent campers and RVers alike and is surrounded by trails, an old fort, and loads of tidepools to explore.

Farther along the route in Sekiu, **Curley's Resort** (360/963-2281 or 800/542-9680, www.curleysresort.com, $48–100 s or d) has nice motel units and cabins with kitchenettes, as well as RV hookups, boat and kayak rentals, a dive shop, and even whale-watching trips through its **Puffin Charters** service.

Also of note is **Winter Summer Inn B&B** (360/963-2264, www.northolympic.com/winters, 75–115 d), with decks overlooking the Clallam River and full breakfasts. The B&B has two rooms with private baths, as well as a separate studio apartment that doesn't include the breakfast.

NEAH BAY

Neah Bay lodging can leave much to be desired. The "resorts" are mostly shoestring operations dependent upon fishermen and hunters who don't mind ancient furnishings and marginally clean rooms. The nicest in-town motel is **The Cape Motel** (360/645-2250, $55–85 d) with rooms including kitchenettes. RV ($24) and tent spaces ($15) are available in summer only.

Washburn's General Store (360/645-2211, 9 A.M.–7 P.M. Mon.–Sat., 9 A.M.–6 P.M. Sun.) sells groceries and has a deli with fresh sandwiches and espresso (this is Washington, after all), plus a small gift shop selling jewelry, baskets, carvings, and knitted items. **Raven's Corner Gifts & Indian Arts** sells local crafts and T-shirts with Makah designs.

Get seafood and burgers at **Warm House Restaurant** (1471 Bay View Ave., 360/645-2924, breakfast and dinner only).

OZETTE LAKE

The Lost Resort (360/963-2899 or 800/950-2899, www.lostresort.net, $50 cabin, $15 campsite) has a general store, deli, camping supplies, showers, and private campsites next to the lake.

Because of overcrowding and resource damage, the Park Service has instituted a **quota system** for overnight hiking in the Ozette area between May 1 and September 30. (There are no restrictions on day use, however.) Make reservations at the Wilderness Information Center in Port Angeles (360/565-3100, www.nps.gov/olym/wic). If you don't have a permit, you might try arriving early to grab one of the 18 campsites accessible by car, but if those are gone, you'll have to drive all the way back to a private campground in Sekiu. The busiest times are weekends in July and August.

The small **Ozette Campground** has camping ($16) year-round, but get here early to be sure of a space (no reservations). The lake is a popular place for boats, canoes, and kayaks, but winds can create treacherous wave action at times. The free **Erickson's Bay** boat-in campground is halfway down the lake on the west side. There is good fishing for largemouth bass, cutthroat trout, kokanee, and other fish here.

Getting There
Clallam Transit (360/452-4511 or 800/858-3747, www.clallamtransit.com) provides daily bus service to Neah Bay and throughout the northern Olympic Peninsula.

Olympic Coast and Hoh Rain Forest

When the highway emerges on the coastline south of Forks, you will quickly become aware that the northern half of Washington's coastline is a picture of how the Pacific coast looks in brochures and calendar photos: pristine beaches, pounding waves, trees sculpted by relentless sea breezes.

Washington's rocky and essentially undeveloped Olympic coast is truly a national gem, and in 1994 it was declared the **Olympic Coast National Marine Sanctuary,** a designation that helps protect the shore and ocean from development. The coast contains rich fishing grounds; more species of whales, dolphins, and porpoises than anywhere on earth; some of the largest seabird colonies in the Lower 48; and an unparalleled beauty that attracts painters, photographers, and anyone with a sense of wonder.

The shore is dotted with cliff-rimmed beaches and forested hills.

Farther inland, you'll encounter a different kind of spectacle—one of mossy trees, gurgling streams, and misty forests. These are the most famous woods in America, the Hoh Rain Forest. Bring your raincoat and a sense of adventure, and prepare to meander.

FORKS
The westernmost incorporated city in the Lower 48, Forks is the economic center and logging capital of the western Olympic Peninsula—a big handle for this town of 3,400 with one main drag. For travelers, the town's big selling point is its proximity to the west side of Olympic National Park and Pacific coast beaches. Also nearby is a modern

moss-draped trees at Hoh Rain Forest

University of Washington natural resources research facility.

Sights

TIMBER MUSEUM

The **Forks Timber Museum** (360/374-9663, 10 A.M.–4 P.M. daily mid-Apr.–Oct., free) has historical exhibits that include a steam donkey, a logging camp bunkhouse, old logging equipment, and various pioneer implements. The real surprise is a large 150-year-old canoe that was discovered by loggers in 1990. Out front is a memorial to loggers killed in the woods and a replica of a fire lookout tower.

BOGACHIEL STATE PARK

Six miles south of Forks on Highway 101, Bogachiel (Native American for Muddy Waters) State Park encompasses 123 acres on the usually clear Bogachiel River. Enjoy the short nature trail through a rain forest, or swim, paddle, or fish in the river—famous for its summer and winter steelhead, salmon, and trout. The park has campsites (360/374-6356, www.parks.wa.gov, $13 for tents, $19 for RV hookups) and is open year-round.

Events

Forks' **4th of July** is actually a three-day festival of fun that includes an art show, pancake breakfast, parades, a loggers show, frog jump, demolition derby, dancing, and fireworks.

Sports and Recreation

Right on the opposite side of the highway from the park entrance is Undi Road, which leads east five miles (the last two are gravel) to the **Bogachiel River Trailhead.** The trail follows the lush, infrequently visited rainforest valley of the Bogachiel River east for two miles through national forest land until reaching the edge of Olympic National Park, where the trail continues all the way up to Seven Lakes Basin (27 miles) or Sol Duc Hot Springs (27 miles). The lower section of trail in the rain forest is a lovely place for a day hike. Mountain bikers are allowed on the trail as far as the edge of the national park, but it's a pretty soggy ride.

FORKS FOR *TWILIGHT* FANS

"City of Forks," a notice in Forks reads, "Population: 3175 Vampires: 8.5." It might seem out of place in this out-of-the-way logging community on the remote Olympic Peninsula. But for those in the know this is just one more sign that this obscure little town has been bitten by *Twilight* fever.

Seemingly overnight, Forks has been overrun with fans of the teenage vampire book series penned by Stephanie Meyer and adapted into a major motion picture released in 2008. Even though Meyer never even visited the town before using it as the setting for her books, the good-natured folks of Fork have had fun with the fame. All around town you'll find *Twilight* t-shirts for sale, signs welcoming fans, menu specials, and even custom-decorated motel rooms. Sightseers will find a red pickup similar to the one driven by the heroine, Bella, parked out front of the visitor's center, and the folks there have teamed up with the local chamber of commerce to offer a special *Twilight* tour of Forks. Included on the tour is a stop in front of Forks High School, where camera crews shot scenes for the movie. For more information, visit www.forkswa.com/HomeofTwilighttheBook.

CAMPING

Camp at **Bogachiel State Park,** four miles south on Highway 101 (360/374-6356, www.parks.wa.gov, year-round $13 for tents, $19 for RV hookups), or at the Park Service's **Mora Campground** (open year-round, $10), 14 miles west of Forks, which offers summertime naturalist programs and nature walks. Dispersed camping (pullouts off the road) is allowed on Forest Service lands throughout Olympic National Forest.

Park RVs at **Forks 101 RV Park** (901 S. Forks Ave., 360/374-5073 or 800/962-9964). Camp for free at Rayonier's **Tumbling Rapids Park** (11 miles northeast of Forks along Hwy. 101, 360/374-6565).

Accommodations

Forks has the most lodging options on the west side of the 101 loop, though some of the motels can leave a little to be desired. The best bet for multi-day stays is to opt for a B&B.

The decor reminds you of a neglected granny's house—faux wood paneling, flowery bedsheets, and spent-looking furniture at **Bagby's Town Motel** (1080 S. Forks Ave., 360/374-6231 or 800/742-2429, www.bagbystownmotel.com, $58–64 d), but the owners are friendly, the gardens outside are pretty, and it is comfortable enough to suffice for a cheap night's stopover while making the Olympic loop.

If you've got the dough, though, upgrade yourself to the **Olympic Suites** (800 Olympic Dr., 1.5 miles north of Forks, 360/374-5400 or 800/262-3433, www.olympicgetaways.com/olympicsuites, $79–119 d) down the road. Here you'll find updated one- and two-bedroom suites with kitchens and free wireless Internet on a nicely wooded property. Pet owners will also find rooms here that accept Rover.

Another very clean motel choice is the **Pacific Inn Motel** (352 S. Forks Ave., 360/374-9400, www.pacificinnmotel.com, $58–89 and up), a basic but newish property that remains well-tended and cares for you with a friendly staff. There aren't a ton of amenities, but you will find coin-op laundry facilities and free coffee and tea in the lobby.

The best choices in town are the bed-and-breakfasts. There are a number of off-the-beaten-path properties ideal for those looking to feel close to the natural surroundings around the town. For example, the **Fisherman's Widow B&B** (31 Huckleberry Lane, 360/374-5693, www.northolympic.com/fw, $125–135 d) is a comfy lodgelike home sitting right on the banks of the Sol Duc river, a favorite among anglers and kayakers who can head right out the back door for their daily adventures. The rooms are spacious and can accommodate up to five people, so adventuring groups can save some cash by sharing.

Also a favorite among anglers, especially fly-fishing fans, is **Brightwater House B&B** (360/374-5453 www.brightwaterhouse.com, $125 d), also on the Sol Duc and which boasts a "liberal" cancellation policy that allows anglers to change their plans when the river conditions change. The common River Room offers great views through its floor-to-ceiling windows.

Historic architecture buffs will best enjoy ◖ **Miller Tree Inn** (654 E. Division, 360/374-6806, www.millertreeinn.com, $110–195 d), a family- and pet-friendly inn that rests inside a well-cared-for 1914 homestead. The downstairs common rooms are especially homey, with rich wood paneling and a living room fireplace. Outside there's a back deck with a large hot tub overlooking the attractive grounds. You can also expect a full farmhouse breakfast.

Food

Meet the loggers over coffee and donuts at **The Coffee Shop** (314 Forks Ave. S, 360/374-6769, 5 A.M.–8 P.M. daily), with friendly waitresses and dependably good food three meals a day.

The In Place (320 S. Forks Ave., 360/374-4004, 6 A.M.–9 P.M. daily) is a good lunch spot, with deli sandwiches and great mushroom bacon burgers. They also serve pasta, steak, and seafood dinners.

A mile north of Forks at the La Push road junction on Highway 101, the **Smoke House Restaurant** (360/374-6258, 11 A.M.–9 P.M. Mon.–Fri., noon–9 P.M. Sat.–Sun.) is open daily for lunch and dinner with wonderful prime rib and a full menu of other all-American faves.

Pacific Pizza (870 Forks Ave. S, 360/374-2626, 11 A.M.–9 P.M. Sun.–Thurs., 11 A.M.–10 P.M. Fri.–Sat.) has the best local pizzas and pasta.

The **Forks Farmers Market** (360/374-6623, 10 A.M.–2 P.M. Fri.–Sat. May–mid-Oct.) takes place next to Sully's Drive-In at the north end of town.

Information and Services

Get local information on the south end of town at the helpful **Forks Chamber of Commerce**

Visitor Center (1411 S. Forks Ave., 360/374-2531 or 800/443-6757, www.forkswa.com, 9 A.M.–5 P.M. daily in summer, 10 A.M.–4 P.M. daily rest of the year).

The **Olympic National Forest and Park Recreation Information Office** (551 Forks Ave. N, 360/374-7566, 8:30 A.M.–12:30 P.M. and 1:30–5:30 P.M. daily in summer, 8:30 A.M.–12:30 P.M. and 1:30–5:30 P.M. Mon.–Fri. the rest of the year) is housed in the transportation building. Stop here for recreation information, maps, and handouts, and to take a look at the big 3-D model of the Olympic Peninsula.

Getting There

Local buses all stop at the transportation building (521 N. Forks Ave.) in Forks. **Clallam Transit** (360/452-4511 or 800/858-3747, www.clallamtransit.com) provides daily service north to Port Angeles and Neah Bay, and west to La Push. Catch the free **West Jefferson Transit** (800/436-3950, www.jeffersontransit.com) bus, south from Forks to Kalaloch, Queets, and Lake Quinault. At Lake Quinault, join the Grays Harbor Transit system for points south and east.

LA PUSH AREA

A 14-mile road heads west from Forks through the Bogachiel/Quillayute River Valley. Nearly all this land has been logged at least once, so be prepared for typical Olympic Peninsula clear-cut vistas. The road ends at La Push, a small village bordering the Pacific Ocean on the south side of the Quillayute River, and the center of the **Quileute Indian Reservation**. The name La Push was derived from the French (*la bouche,* meaning mouth), a reference to the river mouth here. It is an attractive little town with a fantastic beach for surfing and kayaking in the summer or watching storm waves in the winter. Locals have a small fleet of fishing and crabbing boats, a seafood plant, a fish hatchery, and a resort offering simple shoreside accommodations and camping.

Sights

The main attraction at La Push is simply the setting: James Island and other rocky points sit just offshore, and waves break against First Beach. The small **Quileute Tribe Museum** (8 A.M.–3 P.M. Mon.–Thurs., 2–4 P.M. Fri.) housed in the Tribal Center office, has a few artifacts. Ask here for local folks who sell beadwork and other handicrafts, and about ocean and river tours in traditional cedar canoes.

Mora Road branches off from La Push Road three miles east of La Push and provides access to **Rialto Beach** within Olympic National Park. It's pretty easy to tell you've entered public land; instead of clear-cuts, you'll find tall old-growth trees. Mora Campground is here, and the beach is a favorite picnicking area and starting point for hikers heading north along the wild Olympic coast. The town of La Push is just across the wide river mouth to the south.

◖ RIALTO BEACH AREA

This is one of the most popular entry points for the coastal strip of Olympic National Park. Rialto Beach is on the north side of the Quillayute River, just west of the Mora campground and ranger station. The 1.5-mile beach is popular with folks out for a stroll or day hike, but continue northward and the crowds thin out as the country becomes a jumble of sea stacks—remnants of the ancient coast. Hole in the Wall is one of the most interesting of these. This treacherous stretch of shore has claimed many lives, as memorials to Chilean and Norwegian sailors attest. The 21 long and remote miles between Rialto Beach and the Ozette Ranger Station feature abundant wildlife—including bald eagles, harbor seals, shorebirds, and migrating whales at different times of the year. The resident raccoons are here year-round, so hang your food in a hard-sided container!

A popular day hike from the La Push area is **Second Beach,** an easy 0.75-mile trail that starts just south of La Push, followed by 1.5 miles of beach, tidepools, and sea stacks, including a pointed one called the Quillayute Needle. You can camp at a couple of points under the trees, making this some of the most accessible beach camping in the state.

Park at Third Beach, just south of the Second Beach trailhead, for a challenging hike all the way down to **Oil City,** 17 miles away on the north side of the Hoh River. Be sure to carry a tide chart. Oil City neither has oil nor is it a city. Three different exploration parties came here in search of oil—attracted by crude seeping from the ground just north of here. During the 1930s, 11 exploratory wells were drilled and a town was platted, but there simply wasn't enough oil to justify development. A part-paved, part-gravel road leads 11 miles from Highway 101 to the Oil City trailhead.

Clallam Transit (360/452-4511 or 800/858-3747) provides daily bus service to La Push from Port Angeles and Forks. Hikers can catch the bus as far as the turnoff to Rialto Beach and walk or hitch the final three miles.

Events

The unannounced **Surf Frolic Festival** in January attracts surfers and kayakers, but the big event is **Quileute Days** in mid-July, with a tug-of-war, bone games, a fish bake, canoe races, and fireworks.

Recreation
CAMPING

Olympic National Park's **Mora Campground** (open year-round, $10) is a pretty in-the-trees place to pitch a tent. Check with the ranger station here for summertime naturalist programs and nature walks.

RV owners can pull their rigs into **Lonesome Creek RV Park** (360/374-4338, $30–35 full hookups), which offers many sites with ocean views. RVers can also park at nearby **Three Rivers Resort** (360/374-5300, www.northolympic.com/threerivers, $18 with full hookups).

Accommodations

The obvious pick in La Push for lodging, **Quileute Oceanside Resort** (320 Ocean Dr., 360/374-5267, www.quileutenation.com, $45–240 s or d,) offers a range of options, everything from bare-bones camper cabins and simple motel rooms on up to duplex units and brand new cabins facing the breathtaking seastacks.

It is activities central at **Three Rivers Resort** (360/374-5300, www.northolympic.com/threerivers, $59–69 up to 4), which offers guided fishing trips, horseback rides, and float trips at the intersection of La Push and Mora Roads (halfway between Forks and La Push). This pet-friendly establishment is also a good spot to bring Spot.

Manitou Lodge (360/374-6295, www.manitoulodge.com, $139–179 d) is a modern country lodge on 10 acres of forested land off Mora Road. Seven luxurious guest rooms with private baths are $85–125 s or d, including a full breakfast. Also on the property are two cedar-shingle camping cabins ($65–99 d) available spring through fall only. Book up to six months ahead for summer weekends. A gift shop here sells quality baskets, woodcarvings, and beadwork.

Olson's Resort (3243 Mora Rd., 360/374-3142, $80) has space for up to five in a cozy and quiet cabin with a kitchen, just 2.5 miles from Rialto Beach.

Food

There are no restaurants in La Push, but you can get locally famous burgers plus soups and sandwiches east of town at **Three Rivers Resort** (360/374-5300, 11 A.M.–9 P.M.).

Information

The Olympic National Park's **Mora Ranger Station** (360/374-5460) next to the Mora Campground is usually staffed daily June–August, but the rest of the year it's catch-as-catch-can. Stop by for a tide chart and information on hiking along the coast. Rangers offer daily beach walks and short guided hikes, and summer campfire programs on Friday–Sunday nights at the amphitheater.

Getting There

Clallam Transit (360/452-4511 or 800/858-3747, www.clallamtransit.com) provides daily bus service to La Push and other parts of the Olympic Peninsula, transporting you south as far as Lake Quinault, and north to Port Angeles and Neah Bay.

HOH RIVER VALLEY

Heading south from Forks on Highway 101, you pass through the heart of the Olympics and get a taste of the economic importance of logging and how it has changed the landscape. Despite reductions in the amount of timber cut in recent years on Forest Service lands, you're bound to meet a constant parade of trucks laden with logs from private land and reservations.

◀ Hoh Rain Forest

One of Olympic National Park's most famous sights is also one of its most remote. Fourteen miles south of Forks is the turnoff to the world-famous Hoh Rain Forest, located at the end of the paved 19 mile Upper Hoh Road. The road follows the Hoh river through a beautiful valley with a mix of second-growth stands and DNR clear-cuts. Once you enter the park, old-growth stands dominate. The **Hoh Rain Forest Visitor Center** (360/374-6925, 9 A.M.–7 P.M. daily July–Aug., 9 A.M.–4 P.M. daily the rest of the year) offers interpretive exhibits and summertime guided walks and campfire programs. Stop by for brochures, information, books, and educational exhibits on the life of the forest and the climate. It rains a *lot* here; 140 inches of rain per year keep this forest perpetually green and damp under towering conifers over 200 feet tall and up to 10 feet wide. The driest months are July and August.

Two short interpretive trails lead through the lush spikemoss-draped forests behind the visitors center. Lacy ferns carpet the forest floor, and some even survive in the tops of the bigleaf and vine maples. A paved wheelchair-accessible mini-trail is directly behind the center, and the **Hall of Mosses Trail** offers an easy 0.75-mile loop.

Shopping

Five miles up the Hoh Rain Forest Road is **Peak 6 Adventure Store** (360/374-5254, 9:30 A.M.–5:30 P.M. daily) selling all sorts of camping and climbing gear and clothes. The owners are friendly and knowledgeable about local trails, and prices are reasonable.

Sports and Recreation
HIKING
Spruce Nature Trail covers a 1.25-mile loop that crosses a crystalline spring-fed creek and then touches on the muddy, glacially fed Hoh River. More adventurous folks can head out the **Hoh River Trail,** an 18-mile path that ends at Blue Glacier and is used to climb Mt. Olympus. Hikers heading into the wilderness need to pick up permits at the visitors center or the Wilderness Information Center in Port Angeles.

CLIMBING
Climbing the glacier-clad 7,965-foot **Mt. Olympus** is a 44-mile round-trip trek. From the Hoh Ranger Station—the closest and most popular departure point—hike 12 flat miles along the Hoh River Trail, then another five steep ones to the Olympus base camp, Glacier Meadows. Crossing Blue Glacier and the Snow Dome requires rope, an ice ax, crampons, and mountaineering skills; a hard hat is advised because of rock falls near the summit. The eight-mile climb from Glacier Meadows to the summit takes about 10 hours. The best months for climbing are late June through early September, the driest months in the park; prior to that time mud and washouts may slow you down.

Inexperienced climbers and those unfamiliar with the area might be wise to hire a guide to accompany them up to the top. National park guide service contracts change year by year, but one company is a perennial fave: **Mountain Madness** (3018 SW Charlestown St., Seattle, 206/937-8389) runs four-day treks to the top of Olympus meant for beginners on up.

CAMPGROUNDS
The Park Service's ◖ **Hoh Rain Forest Campground,** 19 miles east from Highway 101 at the end of the road, is open year-round with in-the-trees camping for $10. The visi-

tors center has evening naturalist programs in the summer.

The Department of Natural Resources has five small, free, year-round campgrounds near the Hoh River: **Hoh Oxbow Campground** (near milepost 176), **Cottonwood Campground** (two miles west on Oil City Rd.), **Willoughby Creek Campground** (3.5 miles east on Hoh Rain Forest Rd.), **Minnie Peterson Campground** (4.5 miles east on Hoh Rain Forest Rd.), and **South Fork Hoh Campground** (6.5 miles east on Hoh Mainline Rd.). Willoughby Creek is right on the river but has just three sites.

Accommodations
Budget travelers will want to check out the quirky **Rain Forest Hostel** (23 miles south of Forks on Hwy. 101, 360/374-2270, $10 pp, $5 kids). The hostel is out in the sticks and has two dorm rooms with bunk beds, a family room, and a trailer outside for couples. It's closed 10 A.M.–5 P.M., lights out at 11 P.M., and no booze is allowed. Guests are asked to do 15 minutes of chores in the evening or morning before departure. Those without vehicles can catch the West Jefferson Transit bus.

Bring your own bedding to the rustic roadside cabins at **Hoh River Resort** (15 miles south of Forks on Hwy. 101, 360/374-5566, $65 s or d), a quiet property perfect for families and others who may not feel like camping in rain forest country. Tent ($17) and RV ($25) spaces are also here.

Animal lovers will fall head over hoofs for the ◖ **Hoh Humm Ranch** (20 miles south of Forks on Hwy. 101, 360/374-5337, www.olypen.com/hohhumm, $35 s or d), where innkeepers raise a zoo's worth of critters: llamas, strange breeds of cattle, goats, sheep, ducks, geese, rhea birds, and Asian Sika deer. Stay in one of five guest rooms with shared bathrooms at a steal of a rate.

Food
Be sure to bring food if you plan to spend the whole day at the Hoh, as dining options are very limited. Your only option is at the park entrance, where you'll find **Hard Rain Cafe**

(5763 Upper Hoh Rd., 360/374-9288, 9 A.M.–7 P.M. daily), a quiet little mercantile and burger stand that's good for lunches and quick bites on the way in or out of the park.

RUBY BEACH TO KALALOCH

The southern end of Olympic National Park's coastal strip is the most accessible, with Highway 101 running right along the bluff for more than a dozen miles. Short trails lead down to the water at half a dozen points, and at the southern end one finds the town (of sorts) called Kalaloch, with a comfortable lodge, two Park Service campgrounds, and other facilities. Beach camping is not allowed along this stretch of the coast.

Ruby Beach Area

Highway 101 rejoins the coast at Ruby Beach, just south of the mouth of the Hoh River. A very popular trail leads down to beautiful sandy shoreline dotted with red pebbles (garnets, not rubies), with piles of driftwood and the flat top of **Destruction Island** several miles offshore. The island is capped by a 94-foot lighthouse.

The tiny, 400-acre **Hoh Indian Reservation** is a couple miles north of Ruby Beach at the mouth of the Hoh River. A three-mile road leads to the tribal center building (360/374-6582). Stop here to ask about locally made cedar bark baskets, but be ready to pay upward of $200. The village is a trashed, badly littered place, but the ocean views are impressive. On the north side of the river is the area called Oil City, accessible via a partly gravel 11-mile road off Highway 101.

South of Ruby Beach, the highway cruises along the bluff, with five more trails dropping to shoreline beaches, creatively named Beach 1, Beach 2, Beach 3, and so on. A massive western red cedar tree stands just off the highway near Beach 6.

Kalaloch

The bluff and beach called Kalaloch has a campground, gas station/country store, and the **Kalaloch Lodge** (360/962-2271 or 866/525-2562), operated as a park concessionaire. The lodge consists of three different types of facilities: the 1950s-era main lodge ($164 d), cabins of various types ($181–300), and the Seacrest House Motel ($164–186). There are no TVs in the rooms, but the sitting room has one for those who can't miss their soaps. Some of the cabins have kitchens and offer waterside views. Make reservations far ahead for the nicest rooms or the bluff cabins; some places are reserved 11 months ahead of time for July and August. The lodge also has a café, gift shop, and lounge.

Across from the lodge is the Park Service's **Kalaloch Visitor Information Center** (360/962-2283, daily June–Sept., with variable hours the rest of the year) where you'll find natural history books, maps, pamphlets, and tide charts for beach walking.

The National Park Service's **Kalaloch Campground** ($12; open year-round) sits on a bluff overlooking the beach. During the summer, attend campfire programs or join a tidepool walk at Beach 4. The primitive **South Beach Campground** ($8, open summers only) is on the southern edge of the park three miles south of Kalaloch. These are the only two campgrounds on the dozen miles of Pacific shoreline between Queets and the Hoh Reservation.

Queets and Quinault

QUEETS RIVER AREA

South of Kalaloch, Highway 101 crosses the **Quinault Indian Reservation,** where you get to see what clear-cuts really look like. A narrow corridor of Olympic National Park extends along the Queets River, protecting a strip of old-growth timber bordered by cut-over DNR and private lands. The gravel Queets River Road (well marked) follows the river eastward from Highway 101, ending 14 miles later at **Queets Campground.** This free, primitive campground has no running water, but it is open year-round. A seasonal ranger station is also here. The **Queets Loop Trail** departs the campground for an easy three-mile walk through second-growth forests and fields where elk are often seen. Another route, the **Queets Trail,** is more challenging. It requires the fording of Queets River near the campground—wait till late summer or fall for this hike, and use caution—and then continues along the river for 15 miles, passing through magnificent old-growth stands of Sitka spruce. Not for beginners, but an impressive hike.

Olympic Raft & Kayak (360/452-1443 or 888/452-1443, www.raftandkayak.com) leads relaxing float trips down the Queets River each spring.

The Quinault Reservation beaches, from just south of Queets almost to Moclips, have been closed to the public since 1969. However, you can arrange for an escorted tour of Point Grenville or Cape Elizabeth, two good bird-watching spots, by calling 360/276-8211.

The Department of Natural Resources has additional free campsites approximately 14 miles up Hoh-Clearwater Mainline Road. The turnoff is at milepost 147 on Highway 101 (three miles west of the Queets River Rd. turnoff).

◖ LAKE QUINAULT

Surrounded by steep mountains and dense rainforest, Lake Quinault is bordered on the

© ERICKA CHICKOWSKI

Lake Quinault Resort

northwest by Olympic National Park and on the southeast by Olympic National Forest; the lake itself and land to the southeast are part of the Quinault Reservation and subject to Quinault regulations. Located at the southwestern edge of Olympic National Park, Lake Quinault is a hub of outdoor activity during the summer months. This very scenic tree-rimmed lake is surrounded by cozy lodges, and level hiking trails provide a chance for even total couch potatoes to get a taste of the rainforest that once covered vast stretches of the Olympic Peninsula.

The Quinault Rain Forest is one of three major rain forests that survive on the Peninsula; here the annual average rainfall is 167 inches, resulting in enormous trees, lush vegetation, and moss-carpeted buildings. If you arrive in the rainy winter months, bring your heavy rain gear and rubber boots, not just a nylon poncho and running shoes. If you're prepared, a hike in the rain provides a great chance to see this soggy and verdant place at its truest. July and August are the driest months, but even then it rains an average of three inches. Typical Decembers see 22 inches of precipitation.

Sports and Recreation
DAY HIKING
The Quinault area is a hiker's paradise, with trails for all abilities snaking through a diversity of terrain. The 10-mile **Quinault National Recreation Trail System,** accessible from Willaby and Falls Creek Campgrounds and Lake Quinault Lodge, provides several loop trail hiking opportunities along the lakeshore and into the rain forest. Easier still is the half-mile **Quinault Rain Forest Nature Trail,** where informative signs explain the natural features. A good hike for those traveling with small children begins at North Fork Campground, following the Three Lakes Trail for the first mile to **Irely Lake.** The half-mile **Maple Glade Rain Forest Trail** begins at the Park Service's Quinault Visitor Center on North Fork Road.

Another easy jaunt is the **Graves Creek Nature Trail,** a one-mile loop that begins at the Graves Creek Campground on the South Shore Road. From the same starting point, the **Enchanted Valley Trail** takes you through a wonderful rainforest along the South Fork of the Quinault River. Day hikers often go as far as Pony Bridge, 2.5 miles each way, but more ambitious folks can continue to Dosewallips, a one-way distance of 28 miles.

BACKCOUNTRY HIKING
You'll find two across-the-park hikes that begin or end in the Quinault area, one heading northeast over to Dosewallips, and the other heading north over Low Divide to the Lake Elwha area.

The 11,961-acre **Colonel Bob Wilderness** borders the South Shore Road just east of Quinault Lake and has a couple of popular backcountry paths. For an overnight hike, the seven-mile (each way) **Colonel Bob Trail** provides views of Mt. Olympus, Quinault Valley, and the Pacific Ocean from its 4,492-foot summit and passes through impressive rainforests. Drive past Lake Quinault on South Shore Road until you see the trailhead on the right. The two-mile **Fletcher Canyon Trail** doesn't get a lot of use, but it's a fine chance to see virgin timber and a pretty waterfall. The trail starts from South Shore Road just before it enters the park. Access to the wilderness from the south side is via Forest Road 2204, northeast from the town of Humptulips. If you enter from this remote area, be sure to visit the beautiful Campbell Tree Campground (free) and to check out the **West Fork Humptulips River Trail** that departs from the campground.

A 21-mile loop begins near the North Fork Campground, heads up the **Three Lakes Trail** for seven miles to three shallow alpine lakes, and then turns down the **Elip Creek Trail** for four miles before catching the **North Fork Trail** back through dense rainforests to your starting point. An added advantage of this loop is the chance to see the world's largest Alaska cedar, located just off the trail approximately a mile east of Three Lakes.

CAMPING

Choose from seven different public campgrounds in the Lake Quinault area. The Forest Service maintains three campgrounds on the south shore of Lake Quinault: **Falls Creek** (open late May–mid-Sept., $14); **Gatton Creek** (no water, open late May–mid-Sept., $11); and **Willaby** (open mid-April–mid-Nov., $14). Willaby is the nicest of these and has a boat ramp. Olympic National Park campgrounds are more scattered, and all three are open year-round. **July Creek** ($10) is a walk-in campground on the north shore of the lake. **Graves Creek** ($10) is near the end of the South Shore Road, 15 miles from the Highway 101 turnoff. The free **North Fork Campground** is at the end of the North Shore Road. It does not have running water and is not recommended for RVs.

Check out **Rain Forest Village Resort** (516 S. Shore Rd., 360/288-2535 or 800/255-6936, $25 with water and electric hookups) for serene lakefront RV sites. The property is the only campground by the lake with showers on premises, and it also sports a restaurant and general store. Another RV option is **Quinault River Inn** (360/288-2237, $21–25), which is convenient to the gas station and restaurants of Amanda Park.

Accommodations

The rambling **Lake Quinault Lodge** (345 S. Shore Rd., 360/288-2900 or 800/562-6672, www.visitlakequinalt.com, $143–300 d) sits in a magnificent throne of grassy lawns and lakeside shores near the shroud of Quinault's old-growth forests. This is how a lodge should look, with a darkly regal lobby interior and a big central fireplace surrounded by comfortable couches and tables. There are activities galore, with an indoor pool and sauna, lodge-led tours of the Quinault area, and seasonal boat rentals on the property. Inside the rooms, though, the lodge shows its wear as a "classic" lodge with tight quarters and less than luxury furniture that may make some guests feel taken aback by the premium prices. Visitors who go into a stay with the understanding that the premium is for

the location and the history will likely come away much more satisfied than those expecting a four-star resort experience.

Those looking to get a bit more bang for their buck will feel more comfortable in the fireplace cabins offered at **Rain Forest Resort Village** (360/288-2535 or 800/255-6936, www.rainforestresort.com, $149–199 d), just a short way up South Shore Road. This nice little property also sits on the waterfront with its own banked lawns. Cabins are a bit rustic, but updated and roomier than lodge rooms. The resort also has some run-down motel rooms ($95–105 d) that will do in a pinch for those who won't spend much time there. There's also a good restaurant and lounge, a general store, laundry, RV hookups, and canoe rentals on-site. Whether you stay there or not, be sure to wander on the grounds and spot the world's largest Sitka spruce. This thousand-year-old behemoth is more than 19 feet in diameter and 191 feet tall.

For the absolute nicest place in Quinault, you'll have to travel to the other side of the lake. This is the quieter, less-developed side and home to ◖ **Lake Quinault Resort** (314 N. Shore Rd., 360/288-2362 or 800/650-2362, www.lakequinalt.com, $169–199 d), which rents out sparkling clean and very updated townhouse and kitchenette units facing the lake. Units all line up along a picturesque deck overlooking the property's lawn and the lake. This is a primo spot to watch the winds whip up the water in winter or sailboats lazily float by in summer. Across the road, a trail leads to the world's largest western red cedar—63 feet in circumference and 159 feet tall.

Between north and south sides of the road in the little town of Amanda Park, **Quinault River Inn** (8 River Dr., 360/288-2714, $105 d) offers clean and comfortable rooms convenient to the highway and to all of Lake Quinault's destinations. This is a favorite spot of anglers, who enjoy access to launch boats on the Quinault River, which flows behind the property. But new owners have given this place quite a face-lift, so it is nicer than many peninsula motels catering to the fishing and hunting crowd.

Food

Get groceries at the **Mercantile** (352 S. Shore Rd., 360/288-2620, hours vary—call ahead) across the road from Quinault Lodge. The snack bar sells pizzas, burgers, milk shakes, espresso, and sandwiches. Quite good meals are available at **Quinault Lodge** (360/288-2571, entrées $14–20) and just up the road at **Rain Forest Resort** (360/288-2535). The tiny village of Amanda Park on the west end of the lake along Highway 101 has a fine old country store with narrow aisles and sloping wooden floors.

Information and Services

The Forest Service's **Quinault Ranger District Office** (360/288-2525, 8 A.M.–4:30 P.M. daily in summer, Mon.–Fri. the rest of the year), next door to Quinault Lodge on the south side of the lake, gives out informative handouts and offer guided nature walks and talks at the lodge in the summer.

Or stop by the Olympic National Park **Quinault River Ranger Station** (5.5 miles up North Fork Rd., 9 A.M.–5 P.M. daily June–Labor Day, intermittently the rest of the year)

for brochures, maps, and information on the park. The area around the station is a good place to see Roosevelt elk, especially in early summer and after September.

In Amanda Park along Highway 101 you'll find the essentials: a motel, library, church, school, general store, gas station, post office, café, and liquor store.

Getting There

A road circles Lake Quinault, with side routes up both the East and North Fork of the Quinault River for a total of 31 scenic miles. While most of the road is paved, the upper few miles are gravel. This makes a great bike ride. One of the nicest sections is up South Shore Road, which passes scenic **Merriman Falls** and continues through towering old-growth forests to Graves Creek Campground.

West Jefferson Transit (800/436-3950, www.jeffersontransit.com) provides free daily bus service between Forks and Amanda Park. Continue southward from Lake Quinault on **Grays Harbor Transit** (360/532-2770 or 800/562-9730, www.ghtransit.com) to Moclips, Ocean Shores, and Aberdeen.

North Beach

Grays Harbor—one of just three deepwater ports on the West Coast—forms the southern border to the Olympic Peninsula. The northwestern part of the bay and the Pacific Coast north to the Quinault Reservation is commonly called North Beach. Towns included in this 22-mile long stretch of beachfront are Moclips, Pacific Beach, Copalis Beach, Ocean City, and Ocean Shores.

Some commercial development has occurred along this stretch, but the only significant development is Ocean Shores. This resort/residential complex was developed as a summer resort area in the 1960s and '70s and has never become as popular as its developers expected, in part because of the overcast, damp, windy weather, and in part because it lacks the off-

shore rugged beauty of, say, Cannon Beach, Oregon. Still, it is one of the most popular resort areas on the Washington coast.

MOCLIPS TO OCEAN CITY

Two small settlements—Moclips and Pacific Beach—occupy the northern end of the North Beach region, with a handful of stores, lodging places, and cafés. The drive from Moclips south to Ocean Shores marks the transition from the timber-dominated lands of the Olympic Peninsula to beachside resorts. Between Moclips and Copalis Beach, Highway 109 winds along the crest of a steep bluff, with dramatic views of the coastline. From Copalis Beach southward to Ocean Shores, the country is far less interesting and the highway straightens out on the nearly level land. The broad sandy beaches are backed by grassy dunes and fronted by summer and retirement homes. The entire 22 miles of beach between Moclips and Ocean Shores is open to the public, with various vehicle entry points along the way.

The pocket-sized town of Copalis Beach has a cluster of older buildings on the Copalis River, along with RV parks, motels, and gift shops. Ocean City, three miles farther south, is a bit larger, consisting mostly of simple homes set in the trees.

Sights

Crane your neck upward to get a load of the kites afluttering at one of the most popular shoreline parks on the North Shore stretch, **Pacific Beach State Park** (49 2nd St.). Plunked down right in the middle of Pacific Beach's cute village atmosphere, the park offers beach lovers a meandering sandy reach adorned with sea-oat covered dunes. The camping facilities draw in lots of RVing families, making this a great spot for folks looking to get the little ones to socialize.

Just west of Copalis Beach, **Griffiths-Priday State Park** (www.parks.wa.gov) is a quieter day-use facility at the mouth of the Copalis River. This is a birder's delight, as the Copalis Spit here is one of three snowy plover breeding grounds on the Washington coast. Visitors must be mindful, because this endangered species is very sensitive to human intrusion. To protect the plovers, large areas of the beach north of the park entrance are closed to the public—from the high-tide mark to the dunes—between mid-March and late August. The restricted areas are marked on the map at the park entrance. A boardwalk leads to the beach, where you can dig for razor clams below the tide line.

The **Anderson Cabin** (360/289-3842) on the east side of the highway, is open in the summer. Built of beach logs in the 1920s, the cabin contains period furnishings and a display on local author Norah Berg.

Copalis Beach and Ocean City are "Home of the Razor Clam." The State Department of Fisheries sponsors clam-digging clinics (360/249-4628, www.parks.wa.gov) and beach walks throughout the summer at Ocean City State Park to prepare you for the short, intense razor clam season.

Events

The **Chief Taholah Day Celebration** in early July includes arts and crafts, a powwow, salmon bake, canoe races, a parade, and games on the reservation. The **Kelper's Parade & Shake Rat Olympics** is Pacific Beach's festival, featuring two parades on Labor Day weekend. It's followed in mid-September by a **Sandcastle Sculpture Contest** open to everyone.

Ocean City sponsors the area's big 4th of July **Fire O'er the Water** fireworks and picnic, with live music and arts and crafts. In early August, Copalis Beach comes alive with **Copalis Days,** featuring a car parade, street dancing, and food booths. Head to Copalis Beach in mid-September for a popular **Sandsculpture Contest** with contestants of all levels of ability.

Sports and Recreation
CAMPING

The 10-acre **Pacific Beach State Park** (49 2nd St., 360/276-4297 or 888/226-7688, www.parks.wa.gov, $17 for tents, $22 for RVs with hookups, $7 extra reservation fee) in Pacific Beach offers beachfront campsites that put visitors in prime position for early morning beachcombing, kite flying, and sunset watching. The park is open for camping late February to October, and on weekends and holidays the rest of the year.

Ocean City State Park has year-round camping (888/226-7688, www.parks.wa.gov, $14 for tents, $20 for RV hookups, $7 extra for reservations) near the intersection of Highways 109 and 115. Showers are available here.

Copalis has the best selection of RV parks among all for North Shore cities. Settled on the Copalis River near Griffiths-Priday State Park, **Driftwood Acres** (3209 Hwy. 109, 360/289-3484, www.driftwoodacres.com, $30 tent and RV) offers water and electric RV hookups, along with some very nice and private tent sites in the woods. The site has hot showers to clean up after beach play and nature walks. Plus, the free bundle of firewood is a nice touch.

Active families will dig the recreation room at **Riverside RV Park** (6 Condra Rd., Copalis Beach, 360/289-2111, www.riversidervresort. net, $21 full hookup, $16 tent), which includes darts, billiards, and other games. Plus, outside you'll find horseshoe pits, shuffleboard, a playground, and a hot tub. This park is also right next to the Copalis River, so you don't have to wander far in the morning to start fishing; once done, clean up your catch at the clam-and fish-cleaning station. There are showers on-site, plus a convenience store.

Practicalities

You'll find the most dining, lodging, and convenience options in the Moclips and Pacific Beach area. The most RV camping choices fall in Copalis Beach.

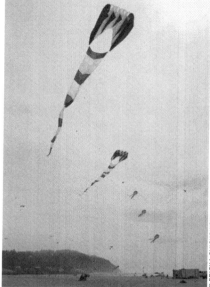

Kites fly aloft at Pacific Beach State Park.

MOCLIPS AND PACIFIC BEACH

Watch the sunset from the veranda at **Moonstone Beach Motel** (4849 Pacific Ave., Moclips, 360/276-4346, www.moonstonemo-clips.com, $99–125 for 4), a simple beachfront property with large kitchenette units that can capably handle families.

The nicest resort in the area is unquestionably ❰ **Ocean Crest Resort** (Moclips, 360/276-4465, or 800/684-8439, $79–209), set on a wooded bluff over Moclips Beach. There's an indoor pool, sauna, hot tub, and exercise rooms, plus the best restaurant in town. The rooms are not luxurious, but they are the best-maintained units north of Ocean Shores. You'll get fireplaces and full kitchens with the pricier rooms. Be sure to reserve far in advance, as this place is not a secret.

Within easy walking distance of Pacific Beach State Park, **Pacific Beach Inn** (12 1st St. S., 360/276-4433, www.pbinn.com, $79–129) provides clean, well-maintained rooms, many with kitchenettes. Furniture is comfy, and many rooms have oceanfront views.

For ocean-view dining, try the excellent

Ocean Crest Restaurant (360/276-4465, 8:30 A.M.–2:30 P.M. and 5–9 P.M. daily) at the Ocean Crest Resort in Moclips. The varied dinner menu features Northwest specialties, steak, and seafood, with weekend entertainment in the lounge. They've got good breakfasts, too. Be sure to ask for a window seat—the views are amazing.

If you rent a unit with a kitchen, pick up supplies at **D and K Grocery** (58 Main St., Pacific Beach, 360/276-4400)

COPALIS BEACH AND OCEAN CITY

Beachwood Resort (3009 Hwy. 109, Copalis Beach, 360/289-2177, $75 s or d) is a summertime pick among families who like the outdoor pool, hot tub, and sauna facilities. Also on premises is a game room and playground for the kiddies. Beach access is pretty limited, though.

Choose among everything from simple motel rooms to full two-bedroom apartments at **North Beach Motel** (2601 Hwy. 109, Ocean City, 360/289-4116 or 800/640-8053,

$45–100 s or d), a bare-bones property perfect for those just lookin' for a roof over their heads and a place to stash their stuff.

Check out **Pacific Sands Resort** (2687 Hwy. 109, Ocean City, 360/289-3588, http://pacific-sands.net, $76 d, $87 up to 4) for a bit more in the amenities department. The property has an outdoor pool, volleyball net, barbecues, a horse corral, and a koi pond. Plus it is dog friendly. Pick between motel rooms with kitchenettes or cabins with full kitchens and fireplaces.

There aren't a whole lot of dining options in Copalis Beach or Ocean City—drive north to Moclips or, better yet, south into Ocean Shores for grub.

Information

Gather information at the **Washington Coast Chamber of Commerce** (2616 Hwy. 109, Ocean City, 360/289-4552 or 800/286-4552, www.washingtoncoastchamber.org, 11 A.M.–5 P.M. Thurs.–Mon. in summer, 11 A.M.–5 P.M. Mon. and Thurs.–Sat., 10 A.M.–2 P.M. Sun. the rest of the year).

Getting There

Grays Harbor Transit (360/532-2770 or 800/562-9730, www.ghtransit.com) has daily service throughout the county, including Moclips to Ocean Shores.

It may not be on your map, but Moclips is connected to Highway 101 by the 20-mile-long Moclips-Quinault Road. Once a rutted and bumpy gravel road, this stretch was recently paved and makes a great shortcut between Quinault and the beaches.

OCEAN SHORES

The summer-home/retirement community of Ocean Shores occupies the six-mile dune-covered peninsula at the north side of the entrance to Grays Harbor. It's an odd place out here, so far from other developments, with a big gate

© ERICKA CHICKOWSKI

Ocean Shores is a favorite among sandcastle "contractors."

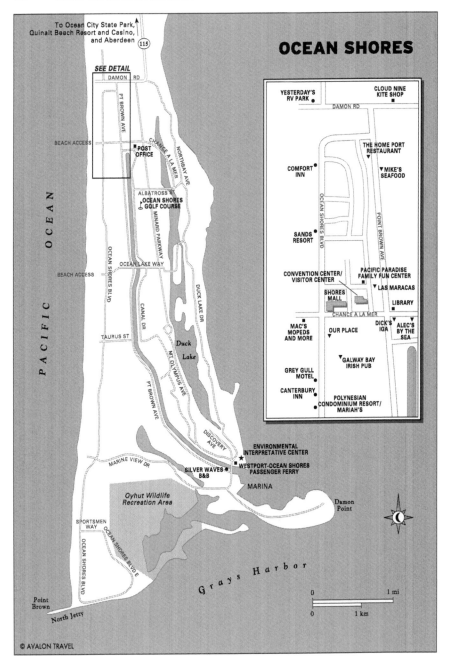

OCEAN SHORES

To Ocean City State Park,
Quinalt Beach Resort and Casino,
and Aberdeen
115

SEE DETAIL

DAMON RD

BEACH ACCESS

POST OFFICE

PT BROWN AVE

CHANCE A LA MER

NORTHBAY AVE

ALBATROSS ST

OCEAN SHORES GOLF COURSE

MINARD PARKWAY

OCEAN LAKE WAY

OCEAN SHORES BLVD

CANAL DR

DUCK LAKE DR

Duck Lake

MT. OLYMPUS AVE

TAURUS ST

PT BROWN AVE

P A C I F I C   O C E A N

BEACH ACCESS

DISCOVERY AVE

MARINE VIEW DR

ENVIRONMENTAL INTERPRETATIVE CENTER
WESTPORT-OCEAN SHORES PASSENGER FERRY
SILVER WAVES B&B
MARINA

Oyhut Wildlife Recreation Area

Damon Point

SPORTSMEN WAY

OCEAN SHORES BLVD

OCEAN SHORES BLVD

Point Brown

North Jetty

Grays Harbor

OCEAN SHORES detail

YESTERDAY'S RV PARK

CLOUD NINE KITE SHOP

DAMON RD

THE HOME PORT RESTAURANT

COMFORT INN

MIKE'S SEAFOOD

OCEAN SHORES BLVD

POINT BROWN AVE

SANDS RESORT

CONVENTION CENTER/ VISITOR CENTER

PACIFIC PARADISE FAMILY FUN CENTER

LAS MARACAS

SHORES MALL

LIBRARY

CHANCE A LA MER

MAC'S MOPEDS AND MORE

OUR PLACE

DICK'S IGA

ALEC'S BY THE SEA

GALWAY BAY IRISH PUB

GREY GULL MOTEL

CANTERBURY INN

POLYNESIAN CONDOMINIUM RESORT/ MARIAH'S

0   1 mi

0   1 km

© AVALON TRAVEL

that welcomes visitors, businesses strewn along a wide main drag, and homes on a network of 23 miles of canals. Some of these homes are elaborate contemporary structures, other lots simply have a concrete pad to park an RV, and many more feature For Sale signs. Many of the working folks live in trailer parks in nearby Ocean City. Two main roads head down the peninsula: the four-lane Ocean Shores Boulevard near the shore, and the bumpy Point Brown Avenue in the center. The latter follows the canals to the marina area. There are no trees on the east side of the peninsula, just low sand dunes.

More than three million visitors come to Ocean Shores annually to play on the beach, fly kites, play miniature golf, and ride bumper cars, bikes, mopeds, and go-karts.

Sights

The **Ocean Shores Environmental Interpretative Center** (five miles south of town center at the marina, 360/289-4617, 10 A.M.–4 P.M. Thurs.–Mon. Memorial Day–Labor Day only) features saltwater and freshwater aquariums and displays on the history of the area, how the peninsula was formed, and how it continues to grow as sand is added each year. Other exhibits detail the animals of the area, and you can watch natural history slide shows.

A pair of wildlife reserves on the southern end of the peninsula offer outstanding **bird-watching**—more than 200 species have been recorded. **Damon Point** (a.k.a. Protection Island) is an important breeding area for the rare snowy plover (this is their northernmost nesting area) and semipalmated plovers (their southernmost nesting area). This is the only place in the world where both species coexist as breeding birds. Parts of the 300-acre preserve are closed March–September to protect the plovers, but the wet sands in the tidal zone are open to fishing and walking. The 682-acre **Oyhut Wildlife Recreation Area** (sometimes spelled Oyehut) at the south end of the peninsula is another good place for bird-watching, with trails through the marshy landscape.

Also on the south end of the peninsula, **North Jetty** reaches a mile out into the Pacific and is a great place to fish, watch storm waves, or enjoy the sunset.

Two miles north of Ocean Shores on Highway 115, **Ocean City State Park** (360/289-3553, www.parks.wa.gov) has campsites close to the town's restaurants and shops. Open year-round, the park has camping in the trees, picnicking, two little ponds for bird-watching, and a path leading through the dunes to the beach. There is no vehicle access here, but there are six access points in Ocean Shores—just head south along Ocean Shores Boulevard and look for the turnoffs. Signs are posted with beach driving regulations and safety warnings. Pedestrians have the right-of-way; cars must yield. Drive only on the higher hard sand, not in the water, on the clam beds, or in the dunes, and observe a 25-mph speed limit. If you get stuck, put boards or other hard, flat material under your tires and pull out slowly. Be sure to hose down your car after driving on the beach, since salt spray can lead to rust.

With all that ocean out there, it's easy to overlook Ocean Shores' six-mile-long **Duck Lake,** but it's a haven for small boats, canoes, anglers (trout, bass, and crappie are all here), swimmers, and water-skiers. You can launch your boat from City Park, at Albatross and Chance à la Mer, or Chinook Park Boat Launch on Duck Lake Drive. At the south end, the lake connects with a maze of canals that lead past housing developments. Pick up a map before heading out, since these channels can be confusing.

Events

Ocean Shores hosts an annual **Beachcombers Fun Fair** at the convention center in early March. See displays of glass floats and driftwood art, and sample the fresh seafood. Ocean Shores' annual **Festival of Colors,** held each May, is family fun with a sandcastle contest, arts and crafts bazaar, and kite festival. The **International Kite Challenge** competition is held out on the beach in the first week of June.

In late July, the leather-jacket crowd rolls into Ocean Shores for the **Harley Owners Group Sun & Surf Run,** an event that attracts 2,000 bikes and riders. The **Dixieland Jazz Festival** in early November features acts from all over the Northwest at the convention center and around town.

Shopping

Ocean Shores' **Shores Mall** has bike and moped rentals, a kite shop, bank, clothing store, and state liquor store on Chance à la Mer, just before the beach. In Homeport Plaza on Point Brown Avenue, Ocean Shores' **Gallery Marjuli** (360/289-2858) is open daily with art and gifts created by Northwest artists. **Tide Creations Gift Shop** (Pt. Brown Ave., 360/289-2550) near the marina has thousands of items, from kites and windsocks to fudge.

Sports and Recreation

Beachcombing is a favorite activity on the six miles of sandy beach along Ocean Shores, as is digging for razor clams in season (generally in March and October). Check with the chamber of commerce for the regulations and where to buy a license.

Rent boats and canoes from **Summer Sails** (360/289-2884) located on the canal at the south end of Point Brown Avenue. Rent mopeds and bicycles at three different places in town: **Mac's Mopeds and More** (798 Ocean Shores Blvd., 360/289-9304), **O. W. W. Inc.** (Shores Mall on Chance à la Mer, 360/289-3830), and **This & That** (748 Ocean Shores Blvd., 360/289-0919).

Ride horseback along the shore on steeds provided by **Chenois Creek Horse Rentals** (360/533-5591). Or, for a unique equine experience, try out the "horse camp" run by **Nan-Sea Stables** (360/289-0194, $60). Adults and kids are all welcome at Nan-Sea's ranch, where you'll learn to care for horses, to properly muck a stall, and take a trail ride during this four-hour long camp.

Ocean Shores is a great place for kite flying, with strong offshore winds much of the year. If you didn't bring your own, head to one of several local kite shops, including **Cutting Edge Kites** (676 Ocean Shores Blvd. NW, 360/289-0667, www.cuttingedgekites.com, 10 A.M.–6 P.M. Mon.–Fri., 9 A.M.–6 P.M. Sat., 9 A.M.–5 P.M. Sun.) and **Cloud Nine Kite Shop** (380 Hwy. 115, 360/289-4424, 10 A.M.–6 P.M. Mon.–Fri., 9 A.M.–8 P.M. Sat., 9 A.M.–7 P.M. Sun.).

At Canal and Albatross in Ocean Shores, **Ocean Shores Golf Course** (360/289-3357) is an 18-hole championship course open to the public.

Pacific Paradise Family Fun Center (767 Minard Ave., 360/289-9537, 11 A.M.–6 P.M. Mon.–Tues. and Thurs.–Fri., 10 A.M.–6 P.M. Sat.–Sun., closed Wed., closed Dec. 1–Dec. 26) has miniature golf, an entertainment center, bumper boats, and more fun options for kids.

CAMPING

One of the only sites in town is **Yesterday's RV Park** (512 Damon Rd., 360/289-9227, $16 tent, $25 full hookup), which offers sites for RVs and tents right on the beach. All sites have fire rings, and there are showers on premises.

Accommodations

Ocean Shores has more than two dozen motels, along with dozens more private home rentals. Note that many places have a two-night minimum on weekends and July–August, and a three-night minimum on holidays. On holidays, the chamber of commerce (360/289-0226 or 800/762-3224, www.oceanshores.org) keeps track of room availability.

UNDER $100

Silver Waves B&B (982 Point Brown Ave. SE, 360/289-2490 or 888/257-0894, $85–130 s or d) has two decks facing the Grand Canal. Four guest rooms and a separate family-friendly cabin all have private baths and a breakfast buffet.

$100-150

Canterbury Inn (643 Ocean Shores Blvd. NW, 360/289-3317 or 800/562-6678, www.canterburyinn.com, $126–150 d) has studios with kitchenettes, along with one- and two-bedroom suites with full kitchens and fireplaces ($204–258 d). The beachfront complex, which has many privately owned units, has a large indoor pool and hot tub. There is a two-night minimum.

$150-200

With its gray-shingled roof in the shape of a stylized gull with its wings spread, the **Grey Gull Motel** (651 Ocean Shores Blvd. SW, 360/289-3381 or 800/562-9712, www.thegreygull.com, $130–195 d) appears (from the appropriate angle) in imminent danger of flying away. The hotel has modern, spacious efficiencies, one- and two-bedroom suites, as well as penthouses ($350 d). There is a two-night minimum on summer weekends. Amenities include a sauna and outdoor pool.

Don't let the brand fool you: The **Comfort Inn** (829 Ocean Shores Blvd., 360/289-9000 or 866/289-9003, $159–279 d) in Ocean Shores is nicer than you'd think—this is a large, upscale place on the beach, with spacious, modern rooms and attentive service. The property includes a pool, fitness center, business center, and continental breakfast.

Situated north of Ocean Shores on land purchased by the Quinalt tribe, **◖ Quinalt Beach Resort and Casino** (78 Hwy. 115, 360/289-9466 or 888/461-2214, www.quinaltbchresort.com, $179 d, $349–549 suites) offers the area's most spacious and comfortable rooms, most with ocean-facing views. Service is very good, and the hotel has a full-service spa with sauna and massage service, walkways out over the dunes to the beach, a nice restaurant, and a café. Plus, of course, there's a full casino.

Polynesian Condominium Resort (615 Ocean Shores Blvd. NW, 360/289-3361 or 800/562-4836, www.thepolynesian.com, $129–229 d) caters to families with its indoor pool, game room, sauna, and hot tub. Choose among hotel rooms, kitchenette efficiencies, or full suites with kitchens and fireplaces. There's a two-night minimum in the summer.

Food

Our Place (676 Ocean Shores Blvd. NW, 360/289-8763, 6 A.M.–2 P.M. daily) is a tiny eatery with inexpensive but filling breakfasts and all-American lunches.

The Home Port Restaurant (857 Pt. Brown Ave., 360/289-2600, 8 A.M.–9 P.M. Sun.–Thurs., 8 A.M.–10 P.M. Fri.–Sat.) serves three meals, including good breakfasts and specialties such as salmon, Dungeness crab, and steak and lobster dinners.

Find very good south-of-the-border meals at **Las Maracas Mexican Restaurant** (729 Point Brown Ave. NW, 360/289-2054, 11:30 A.M.–9 P.M. daily).

Mariah's (615 Ocean Shores Blvd. N.W., 360/289-3315, 4–9 P.M. daily) at the Polynesian Resort is the most upscale local restaurant, with seafood, steak, and pasta, along with a weekend breakfast buffet. The lounge has live music Friday and Saturday evenings.

Alec's by the Sea (131 E Chance à la Mer NE, 360/289-4026, 10 A.M.–8 P.M. Sun.–Thurs., 10 A.M.–9 P.M. Fri.–Sat.) next to Dick's IGA, has low prices and a big menu that includes burgers, fresh clams, salads, steaks, pasta, seafood, and chicken.

Galway Bay Irish Pub (676 Ocean Shores Blvd., 360/289-2300, 11 A.M.–10 P.M. daily) makes great clam chowder.

Mike's Seafood (830 Point Brown Ave. NE, 360/289-0532, 10 A.M.–8 P.M. Mon.–Sat., 11 A.M.–7 P.M. Sun.) sells fresh-cooked crab from a roadside stand.

Get homemade ice cream, fudge, and chocolates from **◖ Murphy's Candy and Ice Cream** (in the Shores Mall, 360/289-0927, 9 A.M.–9 P.M. daily in summer, noon–8 P.M. Mon.–Tues. and Thurs.–Fri., 10 A.M.–8 P.M. Sat., 10 A.M.–6 P.M. Sun.)

Information

Get information from the helpful folks at **Ocean Shores Chamber of Commerce Visitor Information Center** (120B W. Chance à la Mer, 360/289-2451 or 800/762-3224, www.oceanshores.org, 9 A.M.–5 P.M. Mon.–Fri., 10 A.M.–4 P.M. Sat.–Sun.)

Getting There

Grays Harbor Transit (360/532-2770 or

800/562-9730, www.ghtransit.com) has daily bus service throughout the county, connecting Ocean Shores with Aberdeen, Lake Quinault, and Olympia. Ocean Shores has an airport, but no commercial service.

The **Westport-Ocean Shores Passenger Ferry** *El Matador* (360/289-0414, $10 round-trip, free for kids under 4) is a 74-foot passen-

ger boat with service to Westport. Gray whales are often seen along the way. The ferry leaves six times a day and takes 20–40 minutes, with daily service mid-June to Labor Day, and weekends-only service mid-April through mid-June and in September. There is no service the rest of the year. The boat leaves from the marina; get tickets at the Marina Store.

Grays Harbor and Vicinity

Discovered in 1792 by Capt. Robert Gray, an American en route to China to trade sea otter pelts for tea, Grays Harbor is presided over by Aberdeen and Hoquiam (HO-qwee-um). Grays Harbor has long been a major center for the timber industry, and the surrounding country bears witness to this. Heading toward Aberdeen and Hoquiam from any direction leads you through mile after mile of tree farms, with second- or third-growth forests interspersed with newly logged hillsides.

ABERDEEN AND HOQUIAM

Sitting on the easterly tip of Grays Harbor, these twin cities are separated only by the Hoquiam River. Primarily working-class mill towns, they offer weary peninsula and coast travelers a good opportunity to gas up, fill up, and catch some zzz's before hitting the road again. If you stop, be sure to check out the historical sights around town, particularly the Grays Harbor Seaport.

Sights
GRAYS HARBOR HISTORICAL SEAPORT
Captain Gray's discovery of the harbor in the 18th century was only the beginning of what was to become the area's love affair with the sea. The calm waters of the harbor and the ready supply of timber made Aberdeen an ideal shipbuilding headquarters from its early beginnings in the 19th century. Between 1887 and 1920 her port saw off some 130 new ships.

Today the Grays Harbor Historical Seaport (813 West Heron St., Aberdeen, 360/532-8611,

www.historicalseaport.org) highlights the rich maritime heritage of the region, acting as host to two magnificent tall ships. The first, **Lady Washington,** is a full-scale replica of one of the ships in Gray's discovery fleet. This fluttering spectacle of spindly masts and oiled decks carries the honor of sailing as Washington State's Official Ship and is typically in the historical seaport at least two months out of the year along with her companion ship, the **Hawaiian Chieftain,** a steel-hulled, topsail ketch. (The rest of the year they are featured in maritime and tall-ship festivals up and down the West Coast). While in port, *Lady* is open for tours (10 A.M.–1 P.M. daily, $3 adults, $2 seniors and students, $1 children) and offers outstanding three-hour sailing trips most afternoons and weekend evenings ($55 adults, $45 children). The crew is entirely in costume. Schedules change year by year, so be sure to check the Seaport website for up-to-date information.

You might also ask about volunteering aboard the *Lady.* This is not for everyone—simple food, cramped quarters, limited water, and lots of hard work—but at least you aren't subjected to floggings or surgery without anesthesia. No grog either. This is an incredible chance to learn about sailing the old-fashioned way.

MANSIONS AND MUSEUMS
In 1897, lumber baron Robert Lytle built **Hoquiam's Castle** (515 Chenault Ave., Hoquiam, 360/533-2005, 10 A.M.–5 P.M. daily in the summer, 11 A.M.–5 P.M. Sat.–Sun. the

rest of the year, closed in Dec., $4 adults, $1 kids), a stunning maroon-and-white, three-story spectacle that's been restored to its original luster, with the original oak woodwork. It's completely furnished in turn-of-the-20th-century antiques, Tiffany-style lamps, and cut-crystal chandeliers. Half-hour tours are offered throughout the day. The hillside mansion overlooks town and has a distinctive monkey-puzzle tree outside.

Another wealthy lumber magnate, Alex Polson, once owned the largest logging operation in the world, Polson Logging Company (now a part of Rayonier). In 1923 he funded the building of a home for his son and daughter-in-law on property adjoining his own house. This 26-room **Polson Museum** (1611 Riverside Ave., 360/533-5862, www.polsonmuseum.org, 11 A.M.–4 P.M. Wed.–Sat., noon–4 P.M. Sun. Apr. 1–Dec. 23, noon–4 P.M. Sat.–Sun. Dec. 27–Mar. 31, $10 families, $4 adults, $2 students) is now named in his honor. Alex Polson's own home was razed after his death in 1939; his widow didn't want anyone else to live in it. The site of their home is now a small park with a rose garden, historic logging equipment, and a blacksmith shop. The museum houses all sorts of memorabilia: a magnificent old grandfather clock, a fun model railroad, a model of an old logging camp, a two-man chainsaw, and even an old boxing bag.

The **Aberdeen Museum of History** (117 E. 3rd St., 360/533-1976, 10 A.M.–5 P.M. Tues.–Sun., free) displays exhibits of local history, including a century-old kitchen and bedroom, pioneer church, blacksmith shop, four antique fire trucks, a dugout canoe, thousands of pro-union buttons, and a short video about the great fire of 1903 that destroyed 140 buildings. There's lots of offbeat what-was-that-used-for stuff here.

WILDLIFE REFUGE

Due west of Hoquiam off Highway 109, **Grays Harbor National Wildlife Refuge** (360/753-9467, http://graysharbor.fws.gov) is a 500-acre wetland in the northeast corner of Grays Harbor Estuary. This is one of the most important staging areas for shorebirds in North America, attracting up to a million birds each spring. The two dozen shorebird species that visit the basin include the western sandpiper, dunlin, short- and long-billed dowitcher, and red knot; other birds seen here are the peregrine falcon, northern harrier, and red-tailed hawk. A one-mile path leads to the viewing areas, but bring your boots since it's often muddy. The best viewing time is one hour before and one hour after high tide.

Entertainment and Events

The **Driftwood Players,** a community theatrical company, puts on several plays a year at Driftwood Playhouse (120 E. 3rd in Aberdeen, 360/538-1213).

Kick the year off with a fun time at Aberdeen's **Dixieland Jazz Festival,** held on Presidents' Day weekend in mid-February. The **Grays Harbor Shorebird Festival** in late April—the peak of the migration—includes bird-watching field trips and workshops. In early May, the city's **Grays Harbor Discovery Days Celebration** attracts longboats from throughout the Northwest for rowing and sailing races.

Hoquiam's **Loggers Playday,** held the second weekend in September, is an opportunity for sedentary executives to see what real work is all about. After kicking off the event with a parade and salmon barbecue, loggers compete in ax-throwing, log-chopping, and tree-climbing events. Evening brings a big fireworks show.

Sports and Recreation

At E. 9th and N. I Streets, Aberdeen's **Samuel Benn Park** has rose and rhododendron gardens, tennis courts, a playground, and picnic facilities. **Lake Aberdeen** at the east entrance to town has swimming and nonmotorized boating and play equipment. For an indoor pool, head to the **Hoquiam Aquatic Center** (717 K St., 360/533-3474).

CAMPING

Campsites are available at **Lake Sylvia State Park** (360/249-3621, www.parks.wa.gov, open late Mar.–Sept., $9–14 for tents, no hookups) near Montesano, approximately 12 miles east of Aberdeen.

Situated near 20 acres of heavily wooded wilderness, near a creek with catchable crawdads, **Arctic Park** (893 Hwy. 101, Aberdeen, 360/533-4470, http://users.techline.com/articrv/, $22 with full hookups, $10 tents) offers an unusual amount of privacy over the typical corral-type RV park, with vegetation separating many sites. The owners grow a garden with veggies and berries that guests are welcome to pick, and the property includes showers, a volleyball court, and a convenience store. Nearby there's 1.5 miles of trails that run through the forest.

Accommodations

The twin cities of Aberdeen and Hoquiam are less vacation destinations and more convenient stopovers on the way to other points on the peninsula and coast such as Ocean Shores, Lake Quinault, and Kalaloch. Many of the hotels and motels are on the shabbier side of run-down, but there are a few exceptions.

One acceptable choice is the **Guest House Inn and Suites** (701 East Heron St., Aberdeen, 360/537-7460, www.guesthouseintl.com), a clean place that has the only motel pool in town. Guests are invited to munch on a simple continental breakfast each morning.

There are also a couple of very nice bed-and-breakfasts in town. Most impressive among them is the gorgeous **Hoquiam's Castle B&B** (515 Chenault, 360/533-2005 or 877/542-2785, www.hoquiamscastle.com, $145–195 s or d), which features rooms with four-poster beds, claw-footed tubs, and more dainty linens than you can shake a stick at. Breakfast in the morning is an elaborate affair that should sate even the hungriest hikers before heading out into the woods.

Check out some amazing panoramas of the harbor at the colonial revival-style **A Harbor View B&B** (113 W. 11th St., 360/533-7996, www.aharborview.com, $149–225 s or d, no kids under 12). Sitting high on a hill, this bed-and-breakfast offers five bedrooms furnished in Victorian period pieces and colorful

quilts. All rooms include private baths, TVs, and wireless Internet.

Food

In business since 1945, **Duffy's** is the local family restaurant, featuring a varied, inexpensive-to-moderate seafood and steak menu and great blackberry pies. Try this local favorite at two locations, one in Aberdeen (1605 Simpson Ave., 360/532-3842, 6 A.M.–10 P.M. Sun.–Thurs., 6 A.M.–11 P.M. Fri.–Sat.) and one in Hoquiam (825 Simpson Ave., 360/532-1519, 11 A.M.–10 P.M. Tues.–Sat., 11 A.M.–9 P.M. Sun.–Mon.).

Aberdeen's **Breakwater Seafood** (306 S. F St., 360/532-5693, 9:30 A.M.–7 P.M. Mon.–Sat., 11 A.M.–6 P.M. Sun.) is a seafood market/restaurant with good chowder and fresh fish and chips to eat in or take out.

Reservations are recommended for dinner at **Mallard's** (118 E. Wishkah, 360/532-0731, 5–7:30 P.M. Tues.–Sat.), a small place with good quality European-style cuisine prepared by a Danish chef, with daily specialties.

The atmosphere is elegant but not stuffy at **Bridge's** (112 N. G St., Aberdeen, 360/532-6563, 11 A.M.–9 P.M. Mon.–Sat., 4–9 P.M. Sun.), which serves prime rib, steak, and seafood dinners, including razor clams. It is open for lunch and dinner daily plus Sunday brunch.

Billy's Bar & Grill (322 E. Heron, Aberdeen, 360/533-7144, 8 A.M.–10 P.M. Mon.–Sat.) is a restored saloon that serves delicious and reasonably priced steaks, seafood, and burgers.

Decent Italian food and the best local pizzas are at **Casa Mia Pizza** (2936 Simpson Ave., Hoquiam, 360/533-2010, 11 A.M.–midnight Mon.–Thurs., 11 A.M.–1 A.M. Fri.–Sat., 11 A.M.–10 P.M. Sun.).

The **Hoquiam-Grays Harbor Farmers Market** (360/538-9747, 9 A.M.–6 P.M. Tues. and Thurs.–Sat. year-round) takes place at Hoquiam's Levee Park, on the river on Highway 101 North.

Information

The **Grays Harbor Chamber of Commerce and Visitor Center** (506 Duffy St., Aberdeen,

360/532-1924 or 800/321-1924, 9 A.M.–5 P.M. daily) is a good place to find out about the twin cities of Aberdeen and Hoquiam, along with other county towns.

Getting There

Aberdeen and Hoquiam are well served by **Grays Harbor Transit** (360/532-2770 or 800/562-9730, www.ghtransit.com). Buses take you throughout the county seven days a week, including Lake Quinault, Westport, Ocean Shores, and even east to Olympia. **Pacific Transit System** (360/875-9418 or 800/875-9418) provides bus service southward to Raymond, Long Beach, and Astoria, Oregon.

MONTESANO TO OLYMPIA

Zipping up Highway 12 and then Highway 8 on the way to Olympia, this southern link in the Olympic loop is dotted by a few little burgs, including the cozy town of Montesano, which occupies the juncture of the Chehalis, Satsop, and Wynoochee Rivers. The town is home to tidy brick buildings and the hilltop Grays Harbor County Courthouse, built in 1910 of marble and granite. Not far away is the nation's first tree farm, established by Weyerhaeuser in 1941; along Highway 8 you'll whiz by other little hamlets such as Elma and McCleary.

Sights and Recreation

About a mile north of Montesano off Highway 12, **Lake Sylvia State Park** (360/249-3621, www.parks.wa.gov, open late March–Sept.) encompasses 233 acres around this narrow but scenic reservoir. The lake was created by a dam built in 1909 to supply water and power and is a popular place to swim, canoe, or fish. Two miles of trails circle the lake and connect with two more miles of trail in adjacent Chapin Collins Memorial Forest. Be sure to check out the four-foot wooden ball, carved by loggers from a spruce log and used for log rolling until it became waterlogged and sank. The ball was rediscovered in 1974 when the lake level was lowered and is now on display.

Chehalis Valley Historical Museum (703 W. Pioneer Ave., 360/249-5800, noon–4 P.M. Sat.–Sun., free) houses historical logging equipment and century-old photos in what was originally a 1906 church.

Vance Creek County Park, just west of Elma, has nature trails, jogging paths, and swimming in two small lakes. McCleary's **Carnell House Museum** (314 2nd St., noon–4 P.M. Sat.–Sun. Memorial Day–Labor Day only) displays historic photos and a collection of farming, logging, and household equipment from the past.

Festivals and Events

The **Festival of Lights** in December includes a big lighted parade that features everything from logging trucks to cement mixers.

Elma is home to the county fairgrounds, where you can take in an indoor pro rodeo in late March, horse racing in late July, the old-fashioned **Grays Harbor County Fair** in mid-August, and Saturday night auto racing April–September. The **McCleary Bear Festival** in mid-July offers two parades, entertainment, arts and crafts, and food booths. In mid-September, Elma has a **Wild Blackberry Festival** with a pie contest, car show, arts and crafts, and parade.

Practicalities

MONTESANO

Abel House B&B (117 Fleet St. S, 360/249-6002 or 800/235-2235, www.abelhouse.com, $100–130 d) is a historic 1908 home with five guest rooms, Tiffany chandeliers, and attractive grounds. A full breakfast is served.

Lake Sylvia State Park (360/249-3621, www.parks.wa.gov, $9–14) has wooded campsites with no hookups along the shore and is open late March–September. **Lake Wynoochee,** approximately 35 miles north of Montesano, is a popular summertime fishing, hiking, and swimming area within Olympic National Forest. Pitch a tent at **Coho Campground** (353 S. Shore Rd., $10) and hike the scenic 12-mile Wynoochee Lake Shore Trail.

For breakfasts and lunches, the small **Savory Faire** (135 S. Main St., 360/249-3701, www.savoryfaire.com, 10:30 A.M.–3:30 P.M. Mon.–Fri., plus 5:30–8:30 P.M. Fri.) is hard to beat, with a menu that includes omelettes, from-scratch soups, fresh salads, and sandwiches, plus fresh-baked breads, pastries, and espresso to go. Also try **Bee Hive Restaurant** (Main and Pioneer, 360/249-4131, 6 A.M.–8:45 P.M. Mon.–Thurs., 6 A.M.–10 P.M. Fri.–Sat., 7 A.M.–8:45 P.M. Sun.) for all-American meals and homemade pies.

ELMA

The **Grays Harbor Hostel** (6 Ginny Ln., Elma, 360/482-3119, www.ghostel.com, $18 s shared bath, $35 s or d private bath) is a sprawling ranch house situated on eight acres of land. The spotless facilities include an outdoor hot tub, two common rooms, a kitchen, and storage rooms. Blankets and pillows are available, and there's even an 18-hole disc golf course. Open all year, but closed 9 A.M.–5 P.M. daily. Tent space is available for cyclists.

Follow the signs for 12 miles north of Elma to **Schafer State Park** (www.parks.wa.gov, open Apr.–Sept. only, $13 for tents, $19 for RVs) on the Satsop River. Originally a park for Schafer Logging Company employees, today it has public campsites, riverside picnic areas, and a fine collection of mossy trees. There is good fishing for steelhead (late winter) and sea-run cutthroat (summers) in the East Fork of the Satsop River.

MCCLEARY

Built in 1912 and on the National Register of Historic Places, the three-story **Old McCleary Hotel** (42 Summit Rd., McCleary, 360/495-3678, $55–65 s or d) was originally the home of Henry McCleary, for whom the town is named. Today it is owned by Penny Challstedt, who has kept the place as something of a museum, with the original furniture, brass beds, unusual toilets, dark paneling, and Victorian wallpaper. Don't expect a TV or fax machine here. The owner also serves family-style meals, but these are mainly for wedding receptions.

Information

Get local information from the **Elma Chamber of Commerce** (360/482-3055). It is located inside Image Flowers and Fine Chocolates (117 N. 3rd St.).

Getting There

Grays Harbor Transit (360/532-2770 or 800/562-9730, www.ghtransit.com) has daily bus service throughout the county, including Lake Quinault, Westport, Ocean Shores, and east to Olympia.

WESTPORT

Westport, the principal South Beach city, once called itself "The Salmon Capital of the World," and charter services and commercial fishing and crabbing boats still line the waterfront. This is one of the most active ports in Washington, and chain-smoking fishermen drive beat-up old pickups through town. The town also has a crab cannery and several seafood markets, plus the expected waterfront shops offering kitschy gifts, saltwater taffy, and kites. Ragged-at-the-edges Westport is quite unlike its upscale cross-bay twin, Ocean Shores.

Sights

MARITIME MUSEUM

In Westport, the **Westport Maritime Museum** (2201 Westhaven Dr., 360/268-0078, westportwa.com/museum, 10 A.M.–4 P.M. daily June–Sept., noon–4 P.M. Wed.–Sun. Oct.–May, $3 adults, $1 kids) is housed in a magnificent old Coast Guard station built in 1939. Capped by six gables and a watchtower with a widow's walk, the building was used until 1974, when newer quarters were completed just down the road. Inside are photographs of the early Aberdeen–Westport plank road, cranberry and logging industry exhibits, and Coast Guard memorabilia. Out front in glass cases are gray whale, minke whale, sea lion, and porpoise skeletons. Also on the grounds is a building housing the massive lens from the Destruction Island Lighthouse. Built in 1888, it was replaced in 1995 by an automated light. On weekends March–May, the museum offers talks about whales and whale-watching; also check out the interesting video on fish trapping.

PARKS AND BEACHES
Head to the 0.75-mile **South Jetty** at the end of State Park Access Road for a chance to fish, look for birds and marine mammals, or watch the winter storms roll in. Use care on the slippery rocks. The road passes Half Moon Bay, popular with scuba divers. A tall **observation tower** on the east end of Nettie Rose Drive in town provides a fine vantage point to view freighter activity, scenery, sunsets, or an occasional whale, and a lower **ramp tower** on the east end of Nettie Rose looks into the marina. In front of this is a small memorial to fishermen lost at sea.

Entertainment and Events
Westport's **World Class Crab Races & Feed** in mid-April is not a good time to be a crab; the races are followed by a big crab feed. Live music is also featured. The **Blessing of the Fleet,** held annually in May, includes a memorial service for people lost at sea and demonstrations of Coast Guard sea-air rescues. Held in early July, the two-day **Kite Festival** has contests for the youngest and oldest kite flyers, best crash event, longest train of kites, and more. Mid-July has the **Longboard Classic Surf Festival,** attracting top longboard surfers from throughout the Northwest. In August, an **International Nautical Chainsaw Carving Contest** (no, it is not done underwater), and the **Brady's Oyster Feed** both come early in the month.

A very popular event—it's been going on for more than 50 years—is the **Westport Seafood Festival** on Labor Day weekend. Taste salmon, oysters, crab, and all sorts of other fresh-from-the-sea foods, with musical accompaniment.

Sports and Recreation
Open for day use only, **Westhaven State Park** (Hwy. 105 just north of Westport, www.parks.wa.gov) is popular with rockhounds, beachcombers, and divers. Surfers and sea kayakers find some of the most consistent waves in Washington. The jetty was built here to increase the velocity of the seagoing water, collected from six rivers flowing into Grays Harbor. Prior to the construction of the jetty, deposits of sediment mandated annual channel dredging. The jetty worked—the channel hasn't required dredging since 1942.

Westport Light State Park (www.parks.wa.gov), about a mile south of Westhaven off Highway 105 (continue straight when 105 goes left), is another day-use park good for kite flying, rockhounding, and fishing for ocean perch, but no camping. A paved, mile-long **Dune Interpretive Trail** wanders through the dunes, providing several observation platforms that overlook the water. There's vehicular beach access here, but the sand is considerably softer than at other drivable beaches; be careful if you don't have four-wheel drive. Check with the park for regulations on beach driving, since some sections are closed part or all of the year. The classic **lighthouse** inside the park—the tallest on the West Coast—was built in 1898 and is visible from an observation platform on Ocean Avenue. The building is closed to the public, but tours may be offered by the museum. The lighthouse originally stood much closer to the water, but the accretion of sand has pushed the beachfront seaward.

On Highway 105, two miles south of Westport, **Twin Harbors State Park** (www.parks.wa.gov) has campsites, a 0.75-mile sand dune nature trail, picnic areas, and a playground. This is one of the most popular oceanside campgrounds, especially when razor clam harvesting is allowed (usually March and October). Twin Harbors is open for day use all year.

FISHING AND CLAMMING
Even the casual visitor to Westport will see that this is a major sport and commercial fishing port. The harbor is packed with vessels of all dimensions, and charter operators line the marina. You don't have to charter a boat to go fishing; the whole stretch from Westport to North Cove is popular for surf fishing.

The rock jetty near Westhaven State Park is a good spot for catching salmon, rockfish, lingcod, surf perch, and crabs. In September and October, a coho salmon run returns to the marina area (the young are raised in pens here, so this is "home"). Clamming is seasonal and requires a license; see the chamber of commerce for a copy of the regulations. The 1,000-foot-long **Westport Fishing Pier,** off the end of Float 20 at the Westport Marina, is another landlubber fishing option.

Offshore rocks and reefs are feeding grounds for salmon, bottom fish, halibut, and even albacore tuna; take a charter boat to find the best spots, not to mention having your fish cleaned and ready to cook by the time you get back to shore. The charter services all charge about the same amount, so when you call for reservations be sure to check whether the price includes bait and tackle, cleaning, and sales tax, to see if your "bargain" is really a good deal. Note, however, that most departures are at the frightfully early hour of 6 A.M., with a return around 3:30 P.M. Be sure to take along your seasickness pills. Some companies also offer overnight trips that head far offshore in search of tuna. Wander along Westhaven Drive to check out the various charter companies, or get a listing of boats from the visitors center. Expect to pay around $125 per person for halibut charters, $375 for tuna, or $60–75 pp for coho salmon or bottom fishing.

WHALE-WATCHING
Many of the local fishing charter operators provide whale-watching trips March–May, when the gray whales are heading north from their winter quarters off Baja California. Get a list of operators from the visitors center. Expect to pay $20–30 for a three-hour trip. You may also spot whales from the jetty or from the Westport viewing towers. The passenger ferry to Ocean Shores is an inexpensive way to watch for the whales that periodically wander into Grays Harbor. The Maritime Museum offers weekend whale-watching seminars, films, and workshops in season.

SURFING
Surfers can check out the waves at Westhaven State Park, one of the most popular surfing beaches in the state. The man-made jetty here has developed the most consistent point break in Washington, making it well worth braving the icy waters when it is firing. Rent surfboards and wetsuits from the **Surf Shop** (207 Montesano St., 360/268-0992).

KITE FLYING
Cutting Edge Kites (2549 Westhaven Dr., 360/268-0877) has kites and windsocks of every description.

CAMPING
Camp at the very popular **Twin Harbors State Park** (two miles south of town, 888/226-7688, www.parks.wa.gov, $17 tent, $21 full hookups, $7 extra reservation fee). Some campsites are just steps away from the beach, and showers are available. The campground is open late February–October.

Westport is jam-packed with RV parks catering to the fishing crowd. Perhaps the most laden with amenities, **American Sunset Resort** (360/268-0207 or 800/569-2267, www.americansunsetrv.com, $29 full hookups, $19 tent) offers a heated outdoor pool, horseshoe pits and playgrounds, showers, and laundry facilities, plus free Wi-Fi. The property is pet friendly, offers plenty of space for larger rigs, and sports a convenience store and a special area for tent campers. It even rents out two permanent trailers parked at the property.

Accommodations
Most Westport accommodations are straightforward, down-to-earth affairs. Many have kitchenettes, but only a few offer hot tubs or pools. As one owner told me in her broken English, "no pool—big giant ocean out there!" Contact the chamber of commerce (360/268-9422 or 800/345-6223 www.westportgrayland-chamber.org) for a list of rental homes in the Westport area.

Most of the rooms at **Alaskan Motel** (708 N. 1st St., 360/268-9133 or 866/591-4154, www.westportwa.com/alaskan, $60–82 s or d) are simple kitchenette units, though there are some newer guest cottages with enclosed decks ($140–165 d).

A three-story building in the boat basin, **Coho Motel** (2501 N. Nyhus, 360/268-0111 or 800/572-0177) has rooms for $49–54 s or d, and third-floor suites for $68 d. The owners also manage a popular charter fishing operation.

An unpretentious, one-story motel with a gazebo for fresh fish barbecues, **Mariners Cove Inn** (303 Ocean Ave., 360/268-0531 or 877/332-0090, www.marinerscoveinn.com, $59–74 s or d) has clean, modern hotel rooms.

It might fool you at first glance, but **Chateau Westport Motel** (710 Hancock, 360/268-9101 or 800/255-9101, www.chateauwestport.com, $111–124 d, suites $217–383) is actually pretty nice inside. The rooms are comfortable and well equipped, many with balconies and ocean views. The hotel has an indoor heated pool and hot tub. Facilities also include a horseshoe pit and playground, plus free Wi-Fi. As an added bonus, the free continental breakfast starts at the dark hour of 4:30 A.M. for those headed out on fishing trips.

There might not be a pool, but fun-lovin' families will appreciate the go-kart track right on the property at **Breakers Motel** (971 Montesano St., 360/268-0848, www.westportwa.com/breakers, $94–140 d). The motel offers standard rooms and kitchenette units, as well as newer hot-tub suites ($210–230).

Built in 1898 and surrounded by tall evergreens, **Glenacres Inn B&B** (222 N. Montesano St., 360/268-9391 or 800/996-3048, $80–135 d) is the most interesting place to stay in Westport. The B&B has eight guest rooms with private baths, and guests are treated to a full breakfast. A gazebo encloses the hot tub.

Food

Because of the early morning departure of fishing charters, several local cafés are already open when the clock strikes five in the morning. Another recommended lunch place with a salad bar and good seafood is **Barbara's by the Sea** (2323 Westhaven Dr., 360/268-1329, 8 A.M.–6 P.M. Mon.–Thurs., 8 A.M.–8 P.M. Fri.–Sat.) across from the marina. **Las Maracas Mexican Restaurant** (202 W. Ocean Ave., 360/268-6272, 11 A.M.–8 P.M. daily) makes good enchiladas, tostadas, and chimichangas.

You'll find a "surf and turf" menu that includes oysters, halibut, and prawns, along with steaks and pasta, at **King's LeDomaine** (105 Wilson St., 360/268-2556, 7 A.M.–9 P.M. daily).

Buy freshly shucked oysters to go from **Brady's Oysters** (3714 Oyster Place E, 360/268-0077, 9 A.M.–6 P.M. daily). This company was the first to grow oysters on suspended lines, a method that many claim produces a more delicately flavored oyster. You can often buy ultra-fresh fish from commercial fishermen at the marina, and fresh-cooked crab at **Merino's Seafood** (301 E. Harbor St., 360/268-5324, 10 A.M.–6 P.M. daily in summer, 10 A.M.–4 P.M. Sat.–Sun. in winter).

Information

Find maps, brochures, and festival and tour information at the **Westport-Grayland Chamber of Commerce Visitors Center** (2985 N. Montesano St., 360/268-9422 or 800/345-6223, www.westportgrayland-chamber.org, 9 A.M.–5 P.M. Mon.–Fri. year-round, plus 10 A.M.–3 P.M. Sat.–Sun. May–Sept.).

Getting There

Grays Harbor Transit (360/532-2770 or 800/562-9730, www.ghtransit.com) provides daily bus service throughout the county, including Grayland, Aberdeen, Lake Quinault, Ocean Shores, and even to Olympia.

The **Westport-Ocean Shores Passenger Ferry**, *El Matador* (360/268-0047) is a passenger ferry that runs between Ocean Shores and Westport for $8 round-trip (free for kids under 5). The ferry leaves six times a day, with daily service mid-June–Labor Day, and weekend-only service early May–mid-June and in September. There's no service the rest of the year. The ferry departs from Float 10 at the Westport marina.

CRANBERRY COAST

The section of coastline between Westport and North Cove is known as both South Beach and the Cranberry Coast—the former because it is the southern entrance to Grays Harbor, the latter because of the bogs east near Grayland that produce much of the state's cranberry crop. The area is especially popular for sportfishing but also offers long beaches, good surfing, and reasonably priced lodging. The beaches are favorites of post-storm beachcombers who still turn up an occasional glass ball from old Japanese fishing floats.

Sights and Recreation

The crimson crush of cranberry bogs is this quiet region's biggest claim to fame. Visitors can get a roadside tour of the local crop along the aptly named Cranberry Road, as well as Larkin and Turkey Roads. If the tour sparks your interest and you plan on driving farther south, be sure to check out the Cranberry Museum on the Long Beach Peninsula.

A mile south of Grayland on Highway 105, **Grayland Beach State Park** (off Midway Beach Rd., 888/226-7688, www.parks.wa.gov) has 7,450 feet of ocean frontage, 200 acres for picnicking and camping, and a self-guided nature trail through huckleberry, Sitka spruce, and lodgepole pine. This is a popular place to dig for clams. Grayland Beach also has 60 campsites, all with shower access and hookups for $20 ($7 extra for reservations), and is open year-round.

Park RVs at the well-maintained **Kenanna RV Park** (2959 S. Hwy. 105, 360/267-3515 or 800/867-3515, www.kenannarv.com, $25 full hookups, $15 tent)

Entertainment and Events

The third weekend of March, Grayland-area artists display their driftwood and shell creations at the town's **Beachcombers Driftwood Show.** The **4th of July** means a big fireworks display over Booming Bay, and a fun run,

CRANBERRIES

Introduced to Washington in 1883, Cranberries grow on perennial vines in acidic peat bogs and were named by imaginative pilgrims for its flowers that resemble the head and bill of a crane. Today the state produces 16,000 tons of cranberries annually, 4 percent of the nation's total output. Nearly all of the 130 cranberry farms in the state are family-run operations averaging just 11 acres each. They typically sell the crop to Ocean Spray Cranberries, a farmers' cooperative best known for its juice cocktails. It runs two plants in southeast Washington: at Grayland on the "Cranberry Coast" and in Long Beach.

The traditional way to harvest cranberries has been to flood the fields, causing the berries to float to the surface for harvesting. This is still done on some bogs, but most in Washington use dry-harvesting equipment that combs the vines to pull the berries, thanks largely to the Grayland farmer who invented its design.

The most interesting times to visit the cranberry bogs are in mid-June, the peak blooming season, or mid-October, to see the harvest.

arts and crafts, and food booths in Grayland. Early October brings the **Cranberry Harvest Festival** with bog tours, a cranberry cook-off, parade, and dancing.

For some day-to-day excitement, try your luck at **Shoalwater Bay Bingo and Casino** (at the Hwy. 105 turnoff to Tokeland, 360/267-2048 or 888/332-2048, www.shoalwaterbaycasino.com).

Accommodations

Check into **Grayland Motel & Cottages** (2013 Hwy. 105, 360/267-2395 or 800/292-0845, westportwa.com/graylandmotel, $55–93 s or d) and you'll be able to walk out your door to the beach. This family- and pet-friendly facility has a play area for kids and dogs. It also offers complimentary clam guns and shovels to its guests, plus a sink outside to clean them once you catch them.

scenic drive along the Cranberry Coast Scenic Byway

WASHAWAY BEACH

The town of North Cove occupies the northern edge of the entrance to Willapa Harbor; it was once considerably larger. Over the years, the sea has been winning the war with the land, pulling a lighthouse, lifesaving station, canneries, homes, hotels, and schools over the retreating cliff. The shore is now more than two miles back from its position a century ago, a rate unparalleled elsewhere on the Pacific Coast. Although the rate of erosion has slowed, there's often something ready to go over the edge at the aptly named Washaway Beach.

Or try **Grayland B&B** (1678 Hwy. 105, 360/267-6026, $110 s or d) for a homier atmosphere. The proprietors let out two bedrooms with a shared bath in a two-story home built in the 1930s.

A focal point in Tokeland is the wonderfully old-fashioned **Tokeland Hotel** (Kindred Rd. and Hotel Rd., 360/267-7006, www.tokelandhotel.com, $55 s, $65 d). Built as a home in 1885, it became an inn in 1899 and is now on the National Register. The hotel and town are named for Chief Toke, whose daughter married a worker at the lifesaving station here. Together they built a home that was later turned into the Tokeland Hotel. Now on the National Register of Historic Places, it's said to be the oldest resort hotel in Washington, and the spacious front lawn, brick fireplace, and jigsaw puzzles provide an air of relaxation. The restored hotel has upstairs rooms with bath down the hall; reserve several weeks ahead for summer weekend stays. The restaurant, in an open dining room overlooking Willapa Bay, serves three meals a day, specializing in reasonably priced seafood ($10–15 entrées).

Food

Both Grayland and Tokeland are pretty quiet settlements. It makes for nice little getaways, but the drawback is there aren't a whole lot of restaurant options. Most days of the week you can nosh on the comestibles served up at **Mutineer Restaurant** (2120 Hwy. 105, Grayland, 360/267-2077, 8 A.M.–8 P.M. Thurs.–Mon.), which serves all three meals. If you stop by for lunch or dinner, be sure to try some clam chowder.

For those more serious about their seafood, head to **Nelson Crab, Inc.** (3088 Kindred Ave., Tokeland, 360/267-2911, 9 A.M.–5 P.M. daily) for fresh-cooked crab and other seafood for picnics and cookouts.

Information

The small **Cranberry Coast Chamber of Commerce** (2190 Hwy. 105, 360/267-2003 or 800/473-6018, www.cranberrycoast.com) is next to Grandma's Treasure Chest store.

The **Shoalwater Bay Tribe** has a small reservation and tribal offices at Tokeland (Willapa Bay was originally called Shoalwater Bay).

Getting There

Grays Harbor Transit (360/532-2770 or 800/562-9730, www.ghtransit.com) provides daily bus service throughout the county, including Westport, Aberdeen, Lake Quinault, and Ocean Shores.

Long Beach Peninsula

The Long Beach Peninsula is a 28-mile-long strip of sand and fun off the southwestern corner of Washington. Locals call it the "World's Longest Beach," though you're bound to hear disagreement from folks in Australia and New Zealand. Be that as it may, this is one *very* long stretch of sand, and a favorite getaway for folks from Seattle and Portland.

Ask most Puget Sounders who frequent the Long Beach Peninsula what they think about it, and you'll probably get the same protective response Washingtonians have about their state when talking to Californians and North Dakotans: they love it and don't want it to change. The towns on this peninsula have a lived-in look to them, and many of the houses are so sand-peppered and rain-washed that they look as though a designer talked everyone into the weathered-home look. The peninsula is the kind of place where you'll find rubber boots and heavy rain gear on almost every porch—it rains over 70 inches a year here, so be ready to get wet even in the summer—and somewhere in every house is a glass float from a Japanese fishing net and a piece of driftwood.

The central tourist and commercial town on the island, Long Beach has the only walkable downtown area on the coast, with little shops and the typical souvenir joints—like a *real* beach town. At the north end of the peninsula, things are drastically different, with beautifully restored century-old homes in Oysterville, and an isolated natural area at Leadbetter Point.

SIGHTS
◖ Cape Disappointment State Park

Ignore the name—Cape Disappointment State Park (360/642-3078, www.parks.wa.gov) is anything but a letdown. Arguably the most scenic state park in Washington, this 1,882-acre recreational retreat offers dramatic vistas

© WASHINGTON STATE TOURISM/JIM POTH

Cape Disappointment on Washington's southern coast

across the mouth of the Columbia River, old-growth forests, incredible fishing, century-old military fortifications, historic lighthouses, and an impressive museum dedicated to Lewis and Clark.

This is the spot where Meriwether Lewis and William Clark stood in November of 1805, finally having "reached the great Pacific Ocean which we been so long anxious to See." Because game proved scarce and this side of the Columbia lacked protection from winter storms, they crossed the river to build a winter camp called Fort Clatsop near present-day Astoria, Oregon. The fascinating museum at **Lewis and Clark Interpretive Center** (360/642-3029, 10 A.M.–5 P.M. daily) honors the famous duo and is one of the must-see places on Long Beach Peninsula. The interpretive center has enormous windows with expansive views of Cape Disappointment Lighthouse, the Columbia River, and the mighty Pacific.

You can see the mouth of the Columbia by turning right at the concession area and driving to the road's end; park here and walk through the sand to the lookout atop North Jetty. **Cape Disappointment Lighthouse** is the Northwest's oldest, built in 1856; follow the quarter-mile trail from the interpretive center or a steep quarter-mile path from the Coast Guard Station.

The commanding presence and strategic location of Cape Disappointment made it a vital fort location for the new Oregon Territory. The initial cannons arrived in 1862, and **Fort Canby** went on to protect the mouth of Columbia for 95 years. Many of the old bunkers and gun emplacements remain, making for interesting explorations.

Ilwaco

Historic Ilwaco (ill-WOK-o) is a charter, sports, and commercial fishing town on the south end of the Long Beach Peninsula, with docks on protected Baker Bay. The town was named for a Chinook leader, Chief Elowahka Jim. Walk around town to find five murals on the sides of local businesses, and some wonderful old

---

WHAT A LETDOWN

Located at Washington's southernmost point, **Cape Disappointment** earned its name in 1788 from British fur trader John Meares, who was searching for the fabled Northwest Passage. He had heard tales of an enormous river near here from a Spaniard, Bruno Heceta, who had written about it in 1775. Meares failed to find the river (which he hoped would lead to the Passage). The mighty river is surprisingly easy to miss from the sea – Captain George Vancouver also sailed past. The river wasn't officially "discovered" until 1792, when American Capt. Robert Gray sailed his *Columbia Rediviva* into the treacherous river mouth.

---

buildings. Ilwaco's old Fire Station No. 1 on Lake Street contains the "Mankiller," an 1846 hand pumper that was the first fire-fighting apparatus of its kind in Washington Territory. You can view the Mankiller through a window when the building isn't open. Just north of Ilwaco is a pullout along scenic Black Lake; paddleboats are available for rent here in the summer (360/642-3003).

Visit the excellent **Ilwaco Heritage Museum** (115 S.E. Lake St., 360/642-3446, 9 A.M.–5 P.M. Mon.–Sat., noon–4 P.M. Sun. in summer, 9 A.M.–4 P.M. Mon.–Sat. fall–spring) for a look into Pacific Coast history via models, Native American exhibits, and photographs of early settlers' fishing, oystering, and logging methods, along with Cape Disappointment shipwrecks and rescues. Of particular interest is a detailed scale model of the Columbia River estuary, and a display on the *Sector* ($3 adults, $2.50 seniors, $1 children under 12), a 26-foot boat that Gérard D'Aboville rowed from Japan to Ilwaco in 1991.

Washington State Parks conducts tours (360/642-3078, $1) of historic **Colbert House** at the corner of Spruce and Quaker Streets daily in the summer.

Long Beach

Long Beach makes up the commercial core of the peninsula, with all the typical beachfront services, including kitschy gift shops, fish-and-chips takeouts, real estate offices, kite stores, saltwater taffy shops, strip malls, RV parks, motels, and bumper boat, go-kart, and miniature golf amusement parks. Not everything is tacky, but don't come here expecting a classy, romantic experience; this is a family fun-for-all place. In the summer Long Beach hums with traffic and the ringing of cash registers; in winter it slows to a quieter pace but is still popular as a weekend getaway.

Several fine murals grace the sides of buildings in Long Beach. One of the peninsula's most photographed local spots is the **"World's Longest Beach" arch** that rises over Bolsted Street as you head toward the ocean. An elevated and wheelchair-accessible **boardwalk** takes off from here and continues a half mile south to 10th Street; it's a great place for romantic sunset strolls. The gravel **Dune Trail** extends for two miles across the dunes, from 17th Street S to 16th Street N, and is popular with cyclists and hikers.

WORLD KITE MUSEUM

Befitting its beachside location, Long Beach is home to the World Kite Museum and Hall of Fame (3rd St. NW and Pacific Hwy., 360/642-4020, www.worldkitemuseum.com, 11 A.M.–5 P.M. daily May–Sept., 11 A.M.–5 P.M. Fri.–Mon. Oct.–Apr., $5 adults, $4 seniors, $3 children). Inside, you'll learn the history of kites and how they were used during wartime and in developing airplanes. Also here are kites from around the globe, a re-created Japanese kite artist workshop, and a gift shop. The museum offers kite-making workshops the first Saturday of the month May–August.

CRANBERRY ATTRACTIONS

Around 600 acres of cranberries are grown in the Long Beach Peninsula area, and you're bound to see them growing along Highway 101 as you approach the peninsula. Cranberries were originally called "crane berries" by early

---

"CLARK WUZ HERE"

The first Easterners to arrive in Long Beach were the **Lewis and Clark** party, who traveled through this area of sand dunes and pine trees in late 1805, stopping long enough for William Clark to carve his initials on a tree; it's the westernmost point reached by the expedition.

Walking along the Discovery Trail from Ilwaco to Long Beach, you can find a 20-foot bronze statue of a windswept tree memorializing that pine on which Clark cut his mark. Visitors can also check out a life-size bronze statue of the explorers in downtown Long Beach.

---

settlers who thought the blossoms resembled cranes' heads. Ocean Spray Cranberries, Inc. has a processing plant on Sandridge Road in Long Beach, and a second one in Westport. **Anna Lena's Pantry** (111 Balstad Ave., Long Beach, 360/642-8948 or 800/272-6237, 10 A.M.–5 P.M. Mon.–Thurs., 10 A.M.–5:30 P.M. Fri.–Sat., 10 A.M.–4 P.M. Sun.) sells locally made cranberry products.

About a mile northeast of Long Beach is the **Cranberry Museum & Gift Shop** (Pioneer Rd., 360/642-5553, 10 A.M.–5 P.M. Fri.–Sun. May–mid-Dec., free). Operated jointly by the University of Washington and the Pacific Coast Cranberry Research Foundation, the museum shows old and new ways of growing and harvesting cranberries. Visitors can walk the adjacent 10-acre demonstration cranberry bog at any time to learn about this unique crop. Try to time your visit for June, the peak bloom season, or October, to see the harvest.

Ocean Park

Once the Pacific Highway (a.k.a. Hwy. 103) exits the north end of hectic Long Beach, you are suddenly in an almost flat landscape of lodgepole pine trees and scattered summer and retirement homes. You can't see the ocean or Willapa Bay from here, but there are access points all along the way, including at Klipsan Beach. After 11 miles of this, the highway widens into Ocean Park (pop. 1,400), a place considerably more sedate than Long Beach, but nevertheless a popular summer retreat. The **Wreckage,** on the south side of 256th just west of Highway 103, is a unique house constructed in 1912 from logs salvaged after a storm broke apart a raft of logs being towed off the coast. It's on the National Register of Historic Places.

Loomis Lake State Park (south of Klipsan Beach) has picnic tables on the ocean, not the lake; the real Loomis Lake is about a quarter mile north. No camping is allowed here.

◖ Willapa Bay

No matter which way you shuck it, the truth is that the Willapa Bay towns of Nahcotta and Oysterville are quite literally defined by the slurpy sweet meat of the mollusk of love. The latter's name says it all, while the former's namesake is Chief Nahcati, the Native leader who first clued the white man into the oystery bounty of the bay.

The oyster beds are closed to the public, but interpretive signs next to the Nahcotta's Willapa Bay Field Station explain local ecology and the lives of shellfish. **Willapa Bay Interpretive Center** (south side of the Port of Peninsula breakwater, Nahcotta, 360/665-4547, www.opwa.com/interp, 10 A.M.–3 P.M. Fri.–Sun. late May–mid-Oct.) displays exhibits on the oyster industry and the natural history of Willapa Bay.

You can purchase fresh oysters and other seafood in Nahcotta at **Wiegart Brothers Oyster Co., Bendiksen's East Point Seafood Co.,** or the smaller **Hilton's Coast Oyster Company.** Or stop at **Oysterville Sea Farms** (360/665-6585, www.oysterville.net) for fresh or smoked oysters and clams.

A number of homes constructed during the town of Oysterville's heyday have been restored and are now part of the **Oysterville National Historic District.** For a self-guided walking tour map, visit the beautiful white-and-red **Oysterville Baptist Church,** built in 1892.

RISE AND FALL OF OYSTERVILLE

Following the discovery of gold in California, San Franciscans had both gold and a yen to spend it on good food, especially fresh oysters. With oysters selling for up to $50 a plate, the demand led men to search far and wide for new sources. In 1854, Chief Nahcati (the source of the name Nahcotta) showed R. H. Espy and I. A. Clark the rich oyster beds of Willapa Bay. Sensing profit potential, they quickly built the new town of Oysterville on the site, and within a scant few months another 500 boomers had arrived.

The rowdy town grew to become the county seat within two years, and even had a college for a brief period, before overharvesting and winter freezes made the oysters scarce in the late 1880s. With the loss of oysters and the money and jobs they attracted, Oysterville's economy collapsed, and county voters decided to move the Pacific County seat to the logging town of South Bend. Oysterville claimed railroad workers in South Bend had stuffed the ballot box and sued to overturn the vote.

A bitter legal battle ensued that threatened to keep the matter tied up in the courts for years, so a group of South Bend men decided to force the issue. On a Sunday morning in February of 1893, some 85 men crossed to Oysterville abroad two steamships. They first stopped for liquid reinforcement at a local saloon. Then, finding most everyone in church, the mob proceeded to plunder the county courthouse, stealing (or legally removing, depending upon who is telling the story) all the records and furniture. After returning to South Bend with the booty, they sent a bill to Oysterville for services rendered in the process of moving the county records! The county seat has been in South Bend ever since, but the bill was never paid.

On Sunday afternoons in summer the church comes alive with vespers programs featuring an ecumenical mix of secular and religious music.

ENTERTAINMENT AND EVENTS
Nightlife
Every Saturday all summer long, you'll find free concerts in Long Beach's downtown gazebo. Seaview's **Sou'wester Lodge** (360/642-2542) often has concerts, lectures, or poetry on Saturday nights. During the summer and fall, **Nick's West** (1700 Pacific Ave. S, 360/642-5100) has country or rock bands on the weekends.

Festivals and Events
In April, come to Long Beach for the **Ragtime Rhodie Dixieland Jazz Festival.** Then comes Ocean Park's **Garlic Festival,** held the third weekend of June, which features garlic shucking and garlic eating contests, plus all sorts of garlicky meals. Bring a couple of bottles of Listerine along. Long Beach hosts the annual 4th of July **Fireworks on the Beach,** and Ocean Park has a popular **Street Fair** the same weekend. Then comes **Sandsations Sand Sculptures** at the end of the month.

The year's biggest event, the **Washington State International Kite Festival** (www.kitefestival.com) lasts the entire third week of August and draws well over 200,000 spectators and participants. This is the largest kite festival in the western hemisphere, and every day brings a different contest, ending with Sunday's grand finale in which the sky teems with upwards of 4,000 kites of all sorts. The world record for keeping a kite aloft (over 180 hours) was set here in 1982.

Ocean Park hosts an enormously popular classic car show, the **Rod Run to the End of the World,** on the second weekend of September that ends with a 15-mile-long parade. The annual **Cranberrian Fair,** held in Ilwaco in mid-October, celebrates more than a century of coastal cranberry farming. Bog tours give you the chance to see the flooded fields with thousands of floating berries awaiting harvest. It's followed the third weekend of October by **Water Music Festival** with chamber music concerts all over the peninsula.

SHOPPING
It may be campy, but you definitely don't want to miss **Marsh's Free Museum** (409 S. Pacific Ave., 360/642-2188, www.marshfreemuseum.com), a huge souvenir shop in downtown Long Beach. Inside is a delightful collection of the tasteless and bizarre, much of it from old amusement parks, traveling shows, and attics. You'll find an impressive collection of glass fishing balls, the world's largest frying pan, a vampire bat skeleton, an old bottle with a human tapeworm, a gruesome photo of a 1920 triple hanging, and a two-headed calf. Drop a nickel for a flapper-era peep show, pay a dime to test your passion factor on the "throne of love," or search the jam-packed shelves for a stupid postcard, goofy T-shirt, cheap trinket, or bright seashell. Oh, and you won't want to miss "Jake the Alligator Man," stuck in a back corner inside a glass aquarium; he once starred in that arbiter of tabloid discernment, the *Weekly World News*. If you like kitsch, you'll rate this as Washington's finest gift shop! Out front of Marsh's is a small climbing wall ($5 per climb).

The Long Beach Peninsula is one of the best places in Washington for kite flying. Pick up kites, string, supplies and advice at **Above it All Kites** (312 Pacific Blvd. S, Long Beach, 360/642-3541, www.aboveitallkites.com, daily 9 A.M.–5 P.M.).

Wiegardt Studio Gallery (2607 Bay Ave., 360/665-5976, www.ericwiegardt.com, 11 A.M.–4 P.M. Mon.–Fri., 11 A.M.–5 P.M. Sat. July–Aug., 11 A.M.–4 P.M. Fri., 11 A.M.–5 P.M. Sat. Sept.–June) contains the watercolor works of Eric Wiegardt, one of several respected local artists. Wiegart runs numerous art workshops throughout the year, so be sure to check the website for the schedule during your trip.

Shoalwater Cove Gallery (1401 Bay Ave., 360/665-4382, www.shoalwatercove.com, 11 A.M.–5 P.M. daily spring–fall, winter hours vary) has beautifully detailed pastels by Marie Powell.

SPORTS AND RECREATION
Cape Disappointment State Park

North Head Lighthouse was built in 1898 and stands above Dead Man's Hollow, named for the sailors of the ill-fated *Vandelia,* which sank here in 1853. The lighthouse is no longer used; today marine lanterns shine out instead from North Head. The lighthouse is a short walk through the trees from the upper parking lot, or a two-mile hike from McKenzie Head (just west of the campground). Lighthouse tours (360/642-3078, $1) are given daily during the summer. To the south are the dunes and driftwood piles of **Benson Beach** (no vehicles allowed), with Long Beach pointing its finger northward. **West Wind Trail** leads a mile north from the lighthouse through the old-growth forests to Beards Hollow. From there you can continue along the beach all the way to the town of Long Beach, four miles away.

North Head is a favorite place to watch for migrating **gray whales** heading north March–May or south late December–early February. It's also an awe-inspiring place during winter storms when waves pound hard against the rocks below.

Tiny **Waikiki Beach** is a favorite local spot for picnics and swimming in the summer (no lifeguard is present). The beach received its name when a Hawaiian sailor's body washed ashore here after his ship was wrecked in a failed attempt to cross the Columbia River bar in 1811. You can follow a trail uphill from Waikiki to the Lewis and Clark Interpretive Center, and then on to Cape Disappointment Lighthouse.

For a taste of old-growth forests, take the 1.5-mile **Coastal Forest Trail** that begins at the boat ramp along Baker Bay. This is a very enjoyable loop hike.

Cape Disappointment (888/226-7688, www.parks.wa.gov) is one of the most popular places to camp in Washington, welcoming tent ($22)and RV ($31 with full hookups) campers, plus groups of four or less seeking shelter in its permanent yurts ($50 up to six). If you need to clean up, there are coin-operated showers on premises. The campground—within a few yards of beautiful Benson Beach—is open all year.

Leadbetter Point State Park

The northern tip of Long Beach Peninsula is capped by two publicly owned natural areas, Leadbetter Point State Park, and a portion of the Willapa National Wildlife Refuge. Leadbetter has a 1.5-mile trail through the evergreen forest, connecting both parking lots. From the north lot, you can enter Willapa and walk through stunted lodgepole pine forests to beachgrass-covered sand dunes along the Pacific Ocean, or head down to the shore of Willapa Bay for a beach walk. The northern end of Willapa National Wildlife Refuge is closed to all entry April–August to protect the threatened snowy plover that nests on the dunes here. This area is also a very important sanctuary for waterfowl, particularly during spring and fall migrations. Bird-watchers will see thousands (and sometimes hundreds of thousands) of black brant, Canada geese, dunlin, plovers, sandpipers, and other birds in the marshes and beaches during these times. No fires or camping are allowed.

Long Beach

Long Beach is best known for its delightful beach, a favorite of kite enthusiasts. If you don't own a kite, several local shops sell them for all levels of flying ability.

Contrary to expectations, the 28 miles of sandy beach on Long Beach Peninsula are not safe for swimming. Not only are there dangerous undertows and riptides, but rogue waves can occur, and there are no lifeguards. Every year waders or swimmers get trapped in these bitterly cold waters; sometimes the accidents end in tragedy. Locals and visitors looking for a chance to swim generally head to Waikiki Beach, or to local motel swimming pools. Dunes Bible Camp in Ocean Park (360/665-5542, $3) has a large indoor pool open to the public for.

Fishing and Boating

Ilwaco is home to the peninsula's fishing fleet. Some of the more popular excursion companies include **Sea Breeze Charters** (185 Howerton Way SE, 360/642-2300, www.seabreezecharters.net) and **Pacific Salmon Charters** (191

Howerton Way, 360/642-3466, www.pacif-icsalmoncharters.com), both of which lead deep-sea fishing trips off the coast for rock-fish, flounder, sole, lingcod, salmon, and sometimes albacore tuna. They also lead river trips for those in hope of hooking salmon and the Columbia River's mighty sturgeon.

Or stay on shore to fish: More than 230 ships were wrecked or sunk on the Columbia bar before jetties were constructed to control the sand. The longest of these is North Jetty at Cape Disappointment State Park, which reaches a half mile out from the end of the cape and is a popular place to fish for salmon, rock cod, perch, and sea bass.

Stop by the visitors center for a complete listing of local charter operators, along with information on razor clam seasons and harvesting. Clamming is a popular pastime on the sandy stretches of Long Beach. All it takes is a bucket and a shovel, but clam guns can help the success rate. Most people have the best luck about an hour before low tide. Check the Washington State Department of Fish and Wildlife's website (www.wdfw.wa.gov) for information on clamming and fishing seasons and to buy licenses. You can also pick up licenses at **Pioneer Market** (2006 N. Pacific Hwy. 103, Long Beach, 360/642-4004). For fishing supplies, visit **Ed's Bait and Tackle** (207 2nd Ave. SW, Ilwaco, 360/642-2248).

Other Recreation

Rent mopeds, bikes and surreys from **Long Beach Moped** (Sid Snyder Dr., just west of the stoplight at Pacific Hwy. 103, 360/289-3830, 9 A.M.–dark daily Memorial Day–mid-Sept., 9 A.M.–dark Fri.–Sun. the rest of the year).

Horse enthusiasts can rent horses for guided beach rides from **Skipper's Equestrian Center** (S Blvd. and 10th St., 360/642-3676, $25 per hour) or **Back Country Wilderness Outfitters** (10th St. S, Long Beach, 360/642-2576, www.backcountryoutfit.com, $20 per hour).

Two local golf courses are open to the public: **Peninsula Golf Course** (Long Beach, 360/642-2828) and **Surfside Golf Course** (north of Ocean Park, 360/665-4148).

Camping

Great camping for tents or RVs can be had at Cape Disappointment, and RVers will find more than 20 different parking lot/campgrounds along the Long Beach Peninsula. Get a complete listing at the visitors center, or just drive along Pacific Highway until one looks acceptable. For unbeatable oceanfront access, **Andersen's RV Park** (1400 138th St., Long Beach, 360/642-2231 or 800/645-6795, www.andersensrv.com, $45 oceanfront with full hookups, $35 regular full hookups) is the way to go. This dog-friendly park is just a few yards from the sand and surf—grab a fishing pole and tromp through the dune trail to spend the day fishing. There's even a fish-and clam-cleaning station on the property. Facilities also include hot showers and wireless Internet. There are no open fire pits, to preserve the dune grasses, but guests can rent enclosed fire containers ($6/day). Another well-maintained and friendly option, **Driftwood RV Park** (1512 N. Pacific Hwy., 360/642-2711 or 888/567-1902, www.driftwood-rvpark.com, $36 with full hookups) offers grassy sites with lots of space to unwind. Rent a clam gun here to take out to the beach and then use the clam-and fish-cleaning station on premises.

ACCOMMODATIONS

Lodging can be hard to come by on summer weekends, especially during the big festivals. Many rooms are booked a year ahead for Memorial Day weekend, the International Kite Festival in August, and Labor Day weekend. It's a good idea to reserve two to four weeks ahead for other summer weekends. The visitors bureau (360/642-2400 or 800/451-2542, www.funbeach.com) tries to keep track of which accommodations have space. It also has a listing of several dozen vacation houses and cabins available for longer periods of time.

Ilwaco

In Ilwaco, **Heidi's Inn** (126 Spruce St., 360/642-2387 or 800/576-1032, $79–99 s or d) is a tidy, simple little motel that accepts pets.

Owned by the same folks who run the

Shelburne Inn in Seaview, **China Beach Retreat** (222 Capt. Robert Grey Dr., Ilwaco, 360/642-5660 or 360/642-2442, www.chinabeachretreat.com, $215–245) is a lovely 1907 house set amidst an orchard near the mouth of Columbia River. The house is beautifully decorated.

One of the most distinctive local lodging places is at Cape Disappointment State Park, where you can rent one of three historic three-bedroom **Lighthouse Keeper's Residences** (360/642-3078). The head lighthouse keeper's residence ($377) offers the best views of the lighthouse and the mouth of the Columbia, and assistant lighthouse keepers' residences ($267) are nearby. All homes sleep six and feature fully-equipped kitchens and living rooms with TVs and DVD players.

Long Beach

Equipped with a hot tub, sauna, and a small fitness center, **Our Place at the Beach** (1309 S. Ocean Beach Blvd., Long Beach, 360/642-3793 or 800/538-5107, www.willapabay.org/~opat, $52–67 d) has 23 rooms, many with ocean views, each with a fridge. Two larger cabins are also available.

Just across the street from the beach in town, **Anthony's Cabins** (1310 Pacific Hwy. N, Long Beach, 360/642-2802 or 888/787-2754, www.anthonyshomecourt.com, $79–125 s or d) offers studio and one-bedroom units with kitchens in a 1930s-era house.

About a mile north of downtown, **The Breakers** (Hwy. 103 and 26th St., 360/642-4414 or 800/219-9833, www.breakerslongbeach.com, $119–139 s or d) offers pretty standard motel rooms, plus spacious one- or two-bedroom suites with kitchens ($179–278) for up to four. Amenities include an indoor pool, sauna, and hot tub.

For a bit more privacy, try **Boardwalk Cottages** (800 S. Boulevard St., Long Beach, 360/642-2305 or 800/569-3804, www.boardwalkcottages.com, $89–139) with its one- and two-bedroom cottages, many with kitchenettes and decks.

Anchorage Cottages (2209 N. Boulevard St., Long Beach, 360/642-2351 or 800/642-2351, www.theanchoragecottages.com, $80–128) provides beachside units with either one or two bedrooms, most with fireplaces, as well as more spacious two-bedroom cottages with fireplaces. All units have fully equipped kitchens.

There are also several B&Bs right in town. Set within a contemporary home, **A Rendezvous Place Bed and Breakfast** (1610 California Ave. S, Long Beach, 360/642-8877 or 866/642-8877, www.rendezvousplace.com, $129–169 d, suite $219) is one of the rare bed-and-breakfasts that doesn't have so many antiques that you feel like you're in a mausoleum or fear you're going to break something expensive. Rooms are comfy and nicely decorated, and outside there is a hot tub and deck overlooking the private backyard.

Another option is **Boreas B&B** (607 N. Boulevard St., 360/642-8069 or 888/642-8069, www.boreasinn.com, $160–179 s or d), a quiet and cozy 1920s beachfront home with airy and light-colored interiors and an enclosed sundeck with a hot tub. The four guest rooms have shared or private baths. The proprietors also rent out a family- and pet-friendly cottage next door.

Seaview

If you're looking for standard motel accommodations, there are plenty of places along the peninsula, including the immaculately maintained **Coho Motel** (3701 Pacific Hwy., Seaview, 360/642-2531 or 800/681-8153, $45–80 s or d), which provides simple motel rooms with kitchenettes available.

But if you want a friendly place with a funky sense of nostalgia, character, and charm, look no farther than Seaview's **Sou'wester Lodge** (38th Pl., 360/642-2542, www.souwesterlodge.com). Here, literary owners Leonard and Miriam Atkins have created a rustic and offbeat haven for those who appreciate simple comforts. The accommodations include "Bed and Make Your Own Damn Breakfast" rooms in the stately three-story lodge ($119–199 d) built in 1892 as a summer estate by Henry Winslow Corbett, a wealthy timber baron, banker, and U.S. senator from Oregon. Outside are weathered beach cottages ($129–139 d) furnished in "early Salvation Army" decor, and even a hodgepodge of 1950s-era trailers ($69–179 d). Tent and RV space are also available. Artists and writers often "book in" for months at a time, relaxing in this cozy and informal lodge. On many Saturday nights, the sitting room comes to life with lectures, concerts, or poetry. You're likely to find everything from chamber music to discussions on Sufism.

The oldest continuously used lodging in Washington, Seaview's acclaimed **Shelburne Inn** (4415 Pacific Way, 360/642-2442 or 800/466-1896, www.shelburneinn.com, $139–199 d) sits within an elegant 1896 Victorian building. The inn is packed with tasteful antiques, stained-glass windows (from an old English church), and original artwork. TVs would be jarring in such a quaint little place, so don't expect to tune in during your stay. A full country breakfast is included; for many, it's the highlight of their stay. The inn is, however, located just a few feet from busy Pacific Highway, and roadside rooms can be quite noisy. Also beware of the ghost who is rumored to wander the third floor some nights.

Ocean Park

Next to a small pond frequented by ducks and the occasional blue heron is **Shakti Cove Cottages** (1204 253rd Pl., Ocean Park, 360/665-4000, www.shakticove.com, $80–90 d) with 10 cabins nestled in a grove of trees.

Covered in sea-salt-weathered clapboard, **Klipsan Beach Cottages** (22617 Pacific Hwy., Ocean Park, 360/665-4888, www.klipsanbeachcottages.com, $130 d, $155 for 4, $215 for 6) are comfortable older cottages with kitchens and ocean views. This is a quaint place with a lovely meadow on one side and a row of tall pine trees on the other, 200 yards from the beach.

The modern Victorian-style **Caswell's on the Bay B&B** (25204 Sandridge Rd., Ocean Park, 360/665-6535, www.caswellsinn.

com, $160–210) offers friendly and comfortable accommodations facing Willapa Bay. This is a quiet and relaxing place on a three-acre spread. Five guest rooms are furnished with antiques and private baths.

FOOD
Long Beach

In downtown Long Beach, **Cottage Bakery** (118 S. Pacific Ave., 360/642-4441, 4 A.M.–6 P.M. daily) has cabinets filled with sticky-sweet old-fashioned pastries. It's a favorite place for a coffee and dessert while watching the people stroll by.

Dooger's Seafood & Grill (900 Pacific Ave. S, Long Beach, 360/642-4224, daily 11 A.M.–9 P.M.) is a bit formulaic, but is one of the best seafood restaurants in town, with brags about its sourdough bowls full of homemade clam chowder, fish and chips, pan fried oysters, and salads with fresh bay shrimp.

The kiddies will appreciate the pirate-themed **Castaways Seafood Grill** (208 Pacific Ave S, 360/642-4745, www.castawaysseafoodgrille.com), a lively seafood eatery with loads of golden-fried fishies, plus burgers, sandwiches, and salads.

Corral Drive-In (2506 Pacific Ave N, 360/642-2774, 11 A.M.–7 P.M. Mon.–Fri., 11 A.M.–8 P.M. Sat.–Sun.) is another very family-friendly joint. This place is known 'round Washington as the home of the pie-tin sized Tsunami burger—a beast of a sandwich that can literally feed six people. Get the napkins ready, because it sure is messy!

For beef Philly-style, saunter over to **Surfer Sands** (1113 Pacific Ave S, Long Beach, 360/642-7873, 10 A.M.–5 P.M. Sat.–Thurs., 10 A.M.–7 P.M. Fri.), a roadside stand that specializes in ooey-gooey cheese steaks. Summer brings variable extended hours—call ahead.

Seaview

Two Seaview restaurants vie for the breakfast crowds. **Laurie's Homestead Breakfast House** (4214 Pacific Hwy., 360/642-7171, 6:30 A.M.–1 P.M. daily) has a seven-page breakfast menu and very good food. Across the street is **Cheri Walker's 42nd St. Café** (360/642-2323, 8 A.M.–2 P.M. Thurs.–Mon., 9 A.M.–2 P.M. Tues. and 4:30–8:30 P.M. Sun.–Thurs., 4:30–9 P.M. Fri.–Sat.) with traditional American breakfasts, lunches, and dinners. The restaurant features iron-skillet fried chicken, pot roast, steaks, and seafood, with homemade bread and jam, all served in heaping helpings. **Chico's Pizza** (Hwy. 103, right near Sid's Market, Seaview, 360/642-3207) makes tasty pizzas and pastas.

Seaview is also home to one of the peninsula's finest dining options, **The Depot** (38th & L, Seaview, 360/642-7880). Cozied up inside of a restored train station, this creative café plates inventive dishes like grilled wild boar on mashed fava beans and house-made cannelloni stuffed with fresh crab and saffron béchamel sauce.

Ocean Park

The Dunes Restaurant (1507 Bay Ave., Ocean Park, 360/665-6677, 7 A.M.–8 P.M. Sun.–Thurs., 7 A.M.–9 P.M. Fri.–Sat.) serves fresh fish, clam chowder, and Saturday night prime rib. Another good spot to nibble on seafood is **Pilot House Restaurant and Lounge** (1201 West Bay Ave., 360/665-3800, 6:30 A.M.–8 P.M. Sun.–Thurs., 6:30 A.M.–9 P.M. Fri.–Sat.), which serves steaks and pastas along with an ocean view. This is also a convenient spot for country-style breakfasts. In the same building above Pilot House, **Luigi's** (1201 Bay Ave., 360/665-3174, 5–8 P.M. Sun.–Thurs., 4–8 P.M. Fri.–Sat.) bakes up pizza and other Italian classics in a casual setting.

INFORMATION AND SERVICES

Long Beach is the place to go to do your laundry, buy groceries, or get your car washed. Get information at the **Long Beach Peninsula Visitors Bureau** (at the junction of Hwys. 101 and 103, 360/642-2400 or 800/451-2542, www.funbeach.com, 9 A.M.–5 P.M. Mon.–Sat. and 9 A.M.–4 P.M. Sun. in summer, 9 A.M.–4 P.M. Mon.–Sat. fall–spring). Call **Long Beach Info-Line** (800/835-8846) for a recording of current activities, festivals, fun things to do, B&Bs, and more.

The two local **public libraries** are in Ilwaco (158 1st Ave. N, 360/642-3908) and in Ocean Park (1308 256th Pl., 360/665-4184).

GETTING THERE AND AROUND
Getting Around

The Long Beach Peninsula is divided by two parallel main roads: Highway 103, going through the commercial centers on the ocean side, and Sandridge Road, passing the largely residential sections on the bay side. The roads intersect at Oysterville, where only one road continues to Leadbetter Point.

Pacific Transit System (360/642-9418 or 800/642-9418, Mon.–Sat.) has countywide bus service, and dial-a-ride service in certain areas. The system connects with Grays Harbor Transit buses in Aberdeen, and also crosses the bridge to Astoria, Oregon. There is no Greyhound service to the area, and the nearest airport with commercial service is in Astoria. For taxi service, call **Limo Cab** (360/642-4047).

Beach Driving

Approximately 15 miles of Long Beach are open to driving during the summer, but stay on the hard-packed sand, away from the car-eating soft sand and rich clam beds along the water's edge. The sand dunes are off-limits to all vehicles. The maximum speed is 25 mph, and it *is* enforced. If you decide to drive the beach, be sure to wash the salt spray off your car immediately to prevent later rust problems. Check at the visitors center for a current description of areas open to beach driving.

APPROACHING LONG BEACH
From Raymond

Highway 101 continues south from Aberdeen to mill-town Raymond past a patchwork of Weyerhaeuser tree farms and clear-cuts. The winding road can be a traffic nightmare of logging trucks, pokey RVs, and too-few passing lanes. The cops are often out in force here, so don't even think about going over the speed limit.

Continuing south, Washington's coastline wraps around Willapa Bay, the 25-mile-long inlet protected by the Long Beach Peninsula. It is believed to be the cleanest and least developed estuary on the West Coast of the Lower 48 states. Locals posit that these waters produce the best-tasting oysters in the nation (a claim disputed by folks in Grays Harbor and Shelton). Highways 105 and 101 skirt Willapa's scenic marshy shoreline, and tree farms carpet the surrounding hills. This is timber country. A handful of small settlements—notably Raymond and South Bend—offer accommodations and meals.

SIGHTS AND RECREATION

Hikers and cyclists will enjoy the 3.5-mile **Rails to Trails** paved path that follows the river from Raymond to South Bend. Along the way, look for the historic *Krestine,* a majestic, 100-foot sailing ship that plied the North Sea waters for many years.

Follow the signs up the hill to the **Pacific County Courthouse,** built in 1910 and covered by an immense, multicolored stained-glass dome over mosaic-tile flooring. This "gilded palace of reckless extravagance" as it was called, was built at the then-extravagant cost of $132,000, but not everything is as it appears: the marble columns are actually concrete painted to look like marble. A county jail inmate painted the columns and created the decorative panels inside. The courthouse's parklike grounds—complete with a stocked duck pond—offer views of Weyerhaeuser-shaved hills and the town below.

The biggest obstacle to visiting **Long Island** in Willapa Bay is also its biggest asset. This rugged, old-forest-covered island is accessible only by private boat. The muddy tide flats and rich salt grass marshes ringing the island are important resting and feeding areas for migratory waterfowl, and the entire rock is encompassed by the **Willapa National Wildlife Refuge.**

If you can find a means to putt or row out there, you'll have the opportunity to take a stroll through a 0.75-mile trail that meanders through an ancient grove of enormous cedars carpeted with lush mosses.

You don't have to get out to the island to enjoy the wildlife, however; there are numerous turnouts along Highways 105 and 101 where you can pull off and watch herds of elk or black-tailed deer.

Boaters can reach the island from launch areas at refuge headquarters (nine miles west of Naselle and 12 miles north of Ilwaco at 3888 Hwy. 101, 360/484-3482). Before heading to the island, get a map and more information from refuge headquarters. The island has five primitive campgrounds that often fill up on summer weekends (bring your own water, no reservations), but getting there can be tough due to tidal fluctuations—during low tide, you can practically walk out to it.

EVENTS

South Bend's Memorial Day weekend **Oyster Stampede** (360/875-5608) includes oyster shucking and eating contests, wine-tasting, art shows, plus country music and dancing.

RECREATION

Camp along the bay at **Bruceport County Park** (five miles northeast of South Bend on Hwy. 101, 360/875-6611, $10–13 tent, $21 full hookups). Camping and great views across the bay are available nearby at **Bush Pioneer County Park** (2nd and Park, Bay Center, open summers only). Year-round, tenters and RV campers can find respite at **Bay Center KOA** (360/875-6344 or 800/562-7810, $31–36 full hookups, $23 tent), which has showers on-site, plus a playground and a trail to the bay.

PRACTICALITIES

The Russell House B&B (902 E. Water St., 360/875-5608 or 888/484-6907, www.russellhousebb.com, $75–145 s or d) is a beautiful antique-filled Victorian mansion with views of Willapa Bay. The four guest rooms have private or shared baths, a full breakfast is served, and kids are accepted.

If your tummy starts grumbling in Raymond, make it a point to park in front of **Slater's Diner** (124 N. 7th St., 360/942-5109, 11 A.M.–8 P.M. Sun.–Thurs., 11 A.M.–9 P.M. Fri.–Sat.). Fill up on lots of good, ol'-fashioned home cooking and maybe even spot The King in street clothes—one of its staffers moonlights as an Elvis impersonator.

The Boondocks Restaurant (1015 W. Robert Bush Dr., 360/875-5155 or 800/875-5158) is *the* place to eat in South Bend. The specialty, not surprisingly, is oysters, and for breakfast (served anytime) you'll get "hangtown fry," fresh pan-fried Willapa oysters. Also featured are seafood quiche, pastas, veal, and fresh fish.

INFORMATION

Get information about Raymond and South Bend at the **Raymond Chamber of Commerce** (415 Commercial St., 360/942-5419, http://visit.willapabay.org, 11 A.M.–9 P.M. daily).

From Oregon

Most tourists heading from I-5 in Longview and Kelso choose to rumble along the lower Columbia River from the southern Oregon side in order to reach the Long Beach Peninsula. The route along Highway 30 is faster, and it allows visitors to stop off in the unique outpost of **Astoria, Oregon** before heading over the 4.4-mile Astoria-Megler Bridge, the longest continuous-truss span bridge on the continent.

For specifics about Astoria, check out *Moon Oregon* by Elizabeth and Mark Morris. While in Oregon, historical enthusiasts shouldn't miss **Fort Clatsop,** the winter encampment site of the Lewis and Clark expedition, where a reconstructed fort features buckskin-clad park rangers and demonstrations all summer long.

SIGHTS

Just a couple of miles west of the Astoria-Megler Bridge on Highway 101, **Fort Columbia State Park** (360/642-3028, www.parks.wa.gov, 10 A.M.–5 P.M. daily Apr.–Sept.) is a National

Historic Site built in the late 1890s. It, along with Fort Canby and Fort Stephens in Oregon, formed a triad of military bases guarding the mouth of the Columbia. Fort Columbia remained in use through World War II but never engaged in battle. It still has 30 of the original buildings, along with various concrete batteries and two rapid-firing six-inch guns that face out over the mouth of the Columbia. A couple of delightful trails wind through the steep country along the river and an interpretive center in the enlisted men's barracks features two floors' worth of history. History buffs should also make time for the old **Commander's House,** furnished with period pieces.

PRACTICALITIES

Travelers can rent one of two historic guesthouses at Fort Columbia State Park (two miles west of Astoria-Megler Bridge, 360/642-3078, www.parks.wa.gov/fortcolumbia). The first is **Scarborough House** ($268), a restored fort building with accommodations to sleep up to 12 people in four bedrooms, with a full kitchen. The house is named for Captain James Scarborough, who first built a cabin on the land where the fort now stands. Also available is **Steward's House** ($165), a quaint and historic two-bedroom home that sleeps four and has an excellent view of the Columbia River.

This stretch of 101's claim to gastronomic fame is the **Sanctuary Restaurant** (794 Hwy. 101, Chinook, 360/777-8380, www.sanctuaryrestaurant.com, noon–5 P.M. Fri.–Sun.). Housed in a century-old church, the restaurant features fresh seafood and Scandinavian specialties prepared in unusual ways. The desserts are a special treat.

INFORMATION

Pick up information about the lower Columbia River and nearby Long Beach Peninsula at the **Megler Visitor Information Center** (a mile east of the Astoria Bridge on Hwy. 401, 360/777-8388, 9 A.M.–5 P.M. daily May–Sept., 11 A.M.–4 P.M. Fri., 9 A.M.–4 P.M. Sat., 10 A.M.–4 P.M. Sun. Oct.–Nov. and Mar.–Apr., closed Dec.–Feb.), overlooking the river at Megler Cove.

Along Ocean Beach Highway

On the Washington side of the Columbia River, Highway 4 hugs the riverbank for long stretches. This is the road less traveled. Tall cottonwood trees line the riverbanks; high rocky cliffs and Douglas fir trees line the slopes above the highway. As you drive west, the lower Columbia is marked by a series of islands, many little more than sandbars with a fringe of willows and grass. The road banks away from the river at Skamokawa, where it heads toward the sinuous Grays River, which cuts a wide swath, with bucolic farms and fields on both sides and timber country climbing the hillsides.

SIGHTS

The first town you'll encounter after Longview is the little burg of Cathlamet. Stop to visit the small **Wahkiakum Museum** (360/795-3954, 11 A.M.–4 P.M. Tues.–Sun. June–Sept., 1–4 P.M. Thurs.–Sun. Oct.–May, $5 adults, $1 kids), which contains photos and exhibits on early logging practices. Next door is Strong Park and Waterfront Trail. In the park is an unusual geared steam locomotive that hauled logs up steep grades from 1923 to 1958.

Just south of town lies the only populated island in the lower Columbia. Settled by dairy farmers from Switzerland and Scandinavian fishermen, Puget Island offers 27 miles of quiet country roads on rolling hills ideal for a Sunday afternoon drive or bike ride. It is connected to the Washington side by a bridge across the narrow channel, and to Oregon by a small ferry, the *Wahkiakum* ($3 cars, $0.50 passengers, 5 A.M.–10 P.M. daily).

Just west of Cathlamet is the 4,400-acre **Julia Butler Hansen National Wildlife Refuge** (360/795-3915, www.r1.fws.gov), established in 1972 to protect the few remaining Columbian white-tailed deer around the lower reaches of the river. Brooks Slough Road and Steamboat Slough Road circle the refuge, offering a chance to see the small deer sharing grazing rights with dairy cattle and numerous birds, including bald eagles. To protect the deer from disturbance, hiking is prohibited, but you may see them from a blind located at a highway pullout.

Skamokawa's most notable building is **Redmen Hall,** located on a steep bluff overlooking the creek and river. The 1894 schoolhouse was taken over by the Redmen, a fraternal organization that died out in the 1950s. The restored hall is now the **River Life Interpretive Center** (1394 W. Hwy. 4, 360/795-3007, noon–4 P.M. Wed.–Sat., 1–4 P.M. Sun.), featuring historical photos, artifacts, and regional displays. Be sure to stop here and climb the belfry for extraordinary views over the Columbia River estuary.

Follow the signs from Rosburg to the only covered bridge in Washington still in use. The 158-foot-long **Grays River Covered Bridge,** on the National Register, was built in 1905 and covered five years later. The bridge was carefully restored in 1989 and is now a National Historic Landmark. A **Grays River Covered Bridge Festival** is held at the local Grange each August, and includes a parade, crafts booths, music, and a logging contest.

SPORTS AND RECREATION

The best spot to enjoy the recreational opportunities offered by the lower Columbia is in Skamokawa with its quiet estuaries, sloughs and inlets. Launch motorized craft from **Skamokawa Vista Park** (360/795-8605) or wade in at the park's sandy swimming beach (no lifeguard). This is also good place to watch ships crossing the treacherous Columbia River Bar; the busiest time is an hour before or an hour after low tide. When conditions are rough, you'll see enormous swells and waves breaking over these sandbars.

Things are much calmer and more serene along the protected waters of Steamboat Slough, a favorite paddling spot of the guides who lead kayak tours run by **Skamokawa Center** (www.skamokawapaddle.com, $70 one-day tour). The center also offers independent paddlers the chance to rent their own canoes ($40 for two hrs.) or kayaks ($20 two hrs.). Cyclists can also pick up cheap bike rentals ($12 per day) to tour the quiet country roads of Skamokawa, Cathlamet, and Puget Island.

Pitch a tent or pull up small campers halfway

between Longview and Cathlamet at **County Line Park** (2076 E. Hwy. 4, Cathlamet, 360/577-3030, $10 with electric hookups), set right on the river. There are grassy banks for picnicking and plenty of spots to settle down and plunk a line into the water.

Paddlers, RV enthusiasts, tenters, and even those who don't like roughing it too much can find a comfy camping option at the waterfront **Skamokawa Vista Park** (13 Vista Park Rd., 360/795-8605). The park offers simple tent sites ($16), RV hookups ($23), and even yurts ($36–46). Be sure to make a reservation for RV spots and yurts, as this is a popular spot.

Approximately two miles east of Naselle along Highway 4 is the pocket-sized **Salmon Creek Park** in a clump of old-growth forest. Camp here for free under the big trees along Salmon Creek.

PRACTICALITIES

Head into Cathlamet for a solid roof over your head. **Bradley House Inn** (61 Main St., Cathlamet, 360/795-3030, $79–99 d) is set literally on Main Street, offering a small-town America brand of hospitality in a 1907 Eastlake-style home. This former lumber baron mansion offers views of the town, the river, and Puget Island.

You can extend your stay on Puget Island by checking into **Redfern Farm B&B** (277 Cross Dike Rd., 360/849-4108, $55–65 s or d.) where the two guest rooms have a private bath and hot tub. A full breakfast is served, and children are not permitted.

Farther along the route, restored **Skamokawa Inn** (1391 W. Hwy. 4, Skamokawa, 360/795-8300 or 888/920-2777) is the unofficial town square. You'll find a general store, post office, and café at the inn, along with a recreation center that rents kayaks and runs water trail tours. Lodging in the inn ($80 s or $90–95 d) includes a full breakfast. Bring big groups this way—also on the property are apartment and suite rentals sleeping four to 20 ($145–400).

Longview and Kelso Vicinity

The twin blue-collar cities of Longview and Kelso are sandwiched between I-5 and the Columbia River, approximately 40 miles north of Portland. With a long history in fishing and timber, this freeway stopover is a portal to the Long Beach Peninsula 70 miles to the east. It is also a gateway to Mount St. Helens and Portland, Oregon.

SIGHTS

Longview's early planning is revealed by the beautiful **Lake Sacajawea Park,** a 110-acre greenbelt that bisects the city along Nichols Boulevard with a string of serene lakes surrounded by grassy hillsides, shady trees, and a gravel jogging/cycling path.

R. A. Long Park (a.k.a. Civic Center) is a grassy green in the city's core, at the intersection of Olympia and Washington Ways. Surrounding the green are many of the city's oldest buildings, including the wonderful redbrick **Public Library** donated by the town's founder and finished in 1926.

Just up Olympia Way from the Civic Center, the **Nutty Narrows** (600 Louisiana St.) is the world's only sky bridge for squirrels. Builder and developer Amos J. Peters built it in 1963 to save the critters as they attempted to cross the busy street. Peters is honored for his effort with a many-times-greater-than-life-size squirrel sculpture between the library and sky bridge.

Visit the Cowlitz County Historical Museum (405 Allen St., Kelso, 360/577-3119, www.co.cowlitz.wa.us/museum, 9 A.M.–5 P.M. Tues.–Sat., 1–5 P.M. Sun.) to see well-presented Chinook and Cowlitz artifacts, a cabin from 1884, historic photos from the heyday of logging, and changing exhibits.

Lake Sacajawea

ENTERTAINMENT AND EVENTS

The **Columbia Theatre** (1231 Vandercook Way, 360/423-1011), a legacy from the prosperous 1920s, hosts local theater and dance groups as well as national acts. The **Southwest Washington Symphony** (360/425-5346) gives performances there November–April. During July and August, music lovers head to Lake Sacajawea for free Sunday **concerts in the park** featuring everything from tuba fests to country-western bands.

In late June, the **Cowlitz River Canoe Race** is a fast 14-mile river run that starts in Castle Rock and pulls out at Kelso. The Independence Day **Go 4th Celebration** is said to be one of the largest in the country, with a parade, logging show, rubber-duck race, concession stands, and a big fireworks show. In mid-July, the **Summer Arts Festival** attracts artisans from throughout the Lower Columbia. Held at the fairgrounds in late July or early August, the **Cowlitz County Fair** (360/577-3121) has exhibits and entertainment, including the PRCA Thunder Mountain Rodeo. In late August, the

Unique Tin Weekend features old cars, street cruising, and dancing at the fairgrounds.

On the last Sunday of August, the **Three Rivers Air Show** attracts stunt pilots, hang gliders, hot-air balloons, military aircraft, and private planes of all types. The **Kelso Highlander Festival,** held the second weekend of September each year, features a parade, wine festival, art show, rubber-duck race, Scottish bagpipe music, dancing, and food at Tam O'Shanter Park.

SHOPPING

Pick up clothes and other essentials at the sprawling **Three Rivers Mall** (just off I-5 at Longview/Kelso exit 39, 351 Three Rivers Dr. #116, 360/577-5218, www.threeriversmall.com, 10 A.M.–9 P.M. Mon.–Sat., 11 A.M.–6 P.M. Sun.), home of big retailers such as Macy's, JCPenney, Sears, and scores of smaller specialty shops.

Stop by **Broadway Gallery** (1418 Commerce Ave., 360/577-0544, 10 A.M.–5:30 P.M. Mon.–Sat.) to see an outstanding collection of southwestern Washington art produced by more than 30 area artists, including jewelry, pottery, watercolors, weaving, baskets, sculpture, and more.

SPORTS AND RECREATION

Play a round of golf at **Mint Valley** (4002 Pennsylvania, Longview, 360/577-3395, www. mint-valley.com).

If you have a canoe, the Cowlitz River from Castle Rock to Longview is a scenic 16-mile float. The current can be strong and sandbars are visible at low water, but there are no major obstructions along the way.

Windsurfers flock to the Columbia River west and south of Longview, where wind conditions are often perfect for intermediate-level boarders.

Campers will enjoy the lush green lawns and breezy deciduous trees scattered around the pleasant **Brookhollow RV Park** (2506 Allen St., 360/577-6474 or 800/867-0453, www. brookhollow.com, $30 d full hookup, $1 extra for kids and pets), which offers campsites and RV hookups in the heart of Kelso. The closest public camping spaces are at Lewis and Clark State Park, near Winlock.

ACCOMMODATIONS

Built in 1923, **Monticello Hotel** (1405 17th Ave., Longview, 360/425-9900, $60 d) is a redbrick Italianate beauty that still stands as Longview's most elegant structure. The well-appointed luxury suites ($200–250 d) are some of the nicest in the area, and the modest regular rooms in the hotel's adjoining annex are comfortable and reasonable choices for budget travelers. The location can't be beat, as the building faces R. A. Long Park from 17th Avenue.

Sitting on 26 acres outside of town, **Rutherglen Mansion B&B** (420 Rutherglen Rd., 360/425-5816, www.rutherglenmansion. com, $95–125 d) offers three daintily decorated rooms under its English Colonial eaves. Each comes with private bath and fireplace. The hostess serves a full breakfast each morning and spreads a gluttonous Sunday brunch. The restaurant downstairs also serves dinners nightly except Sunday.

Super 8 Motel (250 Kelso Dr., 360/423-8880 or 800/800-8000, www.super8.com, $69 s, $79 d) offers some of the best budget rooms in the area, along with with an indoor pool. **Comfort Inn** (440 Three Rivers Dr., 360/425-4600 or 800/228-5150, $79–109 s or d) is another good chain hotel. The property has an outdoor pool and continental breakfast, plus free Wi-Fi.

For a more personal touch at budget prices, check one of two friendly mom-and-pop motels in town. The **Town House Motel** (744 Washington Way, 360/423-7200, www. townhousemo.com, $50 s, $65 d) offers tidy rooms that include microwaves, fridges, and free high-speed Internet. The property has an outdoor heated pool, and continental breakfast is served each morning.

There's no pool at **Hudson Manor Inn** (1616 Hudson, Longview, 360/425-1100, www. hudsonmanorinn.com, $60 s, $80 d), but the rooms are a little more nicely decorated and also include fridges and microwaves. Hudson has free wireless Internet, plus a free business center and complimentary continental breakfast. The owners here are especially kind.

FOOD

Big breakfast lovers should make haste to give some meaning to the name at **Stuffy's Restaurant** (418 Long Ave., 360/423-6356, 6 A.M.–9 P.M. Mon.–Fri., 7 A.M.–9 P.M. Sat.–Sun.), which features an extensive menu, friendly family service, and enormous servings.

Or nosh on hearty sandwiches and soups, as well as cold smoothies at **Old Creekside Deli** (1323 Commerce Ave., 360/423-7225, 10 A.M.–4 P.M. Mon.–Fri., 11 A.M.–4 P.M. Sat., closed Sun.). Pick up a book at the **Benevolent Bookworm** across the street and plunk yourself down at a courtyard table to read.

Henri's Restaurant (4545 Ocean Beach Hwy., 360/425-7970, 11 A.M.–10 P.M. Sun.–Thurs., 7 A.M.–10 P.M. Fri.–Sat.) is a popular spot for the "power-lunch" business crowd. Specializing in moderately priced salmon or steak dinners and an impressive wine collection, it's open weekdays for lunch, Mon.–Sat. for dinner.

Located in—of all places—the bowling alley, ◖ **Hilander Restaurant** (1509 Allen St., 360/423-1500, 6 A.M.–midnight daily) is a real surprise. This locals' favorite serves great strawberry waffles and big omelettes for breakfast, a salad bar, homemade soups, and tasty halibut fish and chips.

Yan's Chinese Restaurant (300 Long Ave. W, 360/425-3815, 11 A.M.–10 P.M. daily) has reasonable prices and serves up ample portions.

The **Cowlitz Community Farmers Market** (7th and Washington, 360/425-1297, 8 A.M.–1 P.M. Tues. and Sat. April–Oct.) has fruit, flowers, fresh vegetables, honey, bedding plants, berries, and more.

INFORMATION

For information on either Longview or Kelso, contact the **River Cities Chamber of Commerce** (1563 Olympia Way, 360/423-8400, www.rivercitieschamber.com, 9 A.M.–5 P.M. Mon.–Fri.).

The **Kelso Visitors' Center** (just east of the I-5 entrance ramp at 105 Minor Rd., 360/577-8058, 9 A.M.–5 P.M. daily May–Oct., Wed.–Sun. only Nov.–Apr.) provides local information and a small exhibit for those who may have missed the *real* Mount St. Helens visitors centers closer to the mountain. This one has a 15-foot model of the volcano and Toutle River valley, plus photos and exhibits of the 1980 eruption.

GETTING THERE

Community Urban Bus Service (254 Oregon Way, 360/577-3399) provides local service in the Kelso-Longview area Monday–Saturday.

Getaway Express (360/636-5656, $70 one-way) operates shuttle van service between Longview/Kelso and Portland International Airport.

Amtrak (501 S 1st Ave., Kelso, 800/872-7245, www.amtrak.com) trains head north from Kelso to Centralia, Olympia, Tacoma, Seattle, and points beyond, and south to Vancouver, Portland, and California. Service is four times a day. Catch a **Greyhound** (360/423-7380 or 800/231-2222, www.greyhound.com) at the train station (501 S. 1st. Ave.) in Kelso.

MOON THE OLYMPIC PENINSULA

Avalon Travel
a member of the Perseus Books Group
1700 Fourth Street
Berkeley, CA 94710, USA
www.moon.com

Editors: Annie M. Blakley & Shaharazade Husain
Series Manager: Kathryn Ettinger
Copy Editor: Valerie Sellers Blanton
Graphics Coordinator: Kathryn Osgood
Production Coordinator: Domini Dragoone
Cover Designer: Domini Dragoone
Map Editor: Brice Ticen
Cartographers: Jon Twena, Lohnes & Wright,
   Kat Bennett
Contributing Writer: Paul Chickowski

ISBN-13: 978-1-59880-271-9

Some photos and illustrations are used by permission and are the property of the original copyright owners.

Front cover photo: Madison Falls in Olympic National Park © dreamstime.com.
Title page photo: HOH Rainforest trees, © wikimedia.org.

Printed in the United States

ABOUT THE AUTHOR

Ericka Chickowski

When Ericka Chickowski was a kid, her parents told her she had too many recreational interests. Little did they know these would serve her well in her career as a freelance writer. Over the better half of a decade, she has covered everything from river rafting to llama trekking. Ericka's travel stories have appeared on the pages of publications such as *The Seattle Post-Intelligencer, Alaska Airlines Magazine*, and *Midwest Airlines Magazine*. She is also a respected technology journalist who has garnered awards from the Society of Professional Journalists for column, feature, and humor writing.

Ericka grew up under the shade of Washington's evergreens. She learned to appreciate the state's diverse landscape from the backseat of a minivan during family road trips. Once she learned to drive herself, her wanderlust and love for the outdoors sent her on a lifelong quest to explore the nooks and crannies of the state, from the windswept plateaus of dry Eastern Washington to the mossy rainforests of the Olympic Peninsula. In spite of her appreciation for nature, she still thinks one of the prettiest views of Mt. Rainier is from Red Square at the Seattle campus of University of Washington, her alma mater.

Though Ericka settled down several years ago in a San Diego beach cottage with her husband, Paul, and her lovable mutt, Sandy, she regularly visits the trails, museums and restaurants of her home state. In fact, during the course of her research for this book she logged more than 2,000 miles along Washington's highways and byways. Her quest to find the coolest roadside eateries, the funkiest museums, and the grandest vistas keeps her coming back time and again.

14711394R00055

Made in the USA
Lexington, KY
16 April 2012